Tell It Slant

AN ANTHOLOGY OF CREATIVE NONFICTION
BY WRITERS FROM COLORADO'S PRISONS

Facilitated by the University Of Denver's
Prison Arts Initiative

Supported by the
Colorado Department Of Corrections

Table of Contents

Buena Vista Minimum Center

Colorado State Penitentiary

Colorado Territorial Correctional Facility

Denver Reception and Diagnostic Center

Denver Women's Correctional Facility

Four Mile Correctional Facility

Fremont Correctional Facility

Limon Correctional Facility

Sterling Correctional Facility

Introduction

In a time of unprecedented isolation, the stories we tell ourselves and each other create a sense of community, of belonging. The writings in this anthology come from a correspondence course, Tell it Slant: Reading & Writing Creative Nonfiction, that the University of Denver's Prison Arts Initiative (DU PAI) offered in collaboration with the Colorado Department of Corrections (CDOC) at nine state facilities. As we designed the course, which would be offered in the midst of the Coronavirus pandemic, we knew that we wanted to focus on the power of telling our truths as a means to feel connected to each other. We also knew that we wanted to highlight the power of brevity, with flash nonfiction allowing a piece to focus on one movement or image, one moment in time or one corner of space. This focus, zooming in to a single experience, creates an invitation to truly grasp something (sometimes for the first time), including how that thing is connected to so many others. One paradox of this mode of writing is that its predilection towards conciseness and particularity often reveals something about the bigness and manifoldness of the world.

The words "creative" and "nonfiction" describe the form. The word "creative" does not mean, we told our students, that we pretend or exaggerate or make up facts and embellish details, simply that we use the literary techniques often found in fiction and poetry to tell the truth. The goal of creative nonfiction is to tell true stories as well as we can.

A dedicated group of individuals—consisting of students, teachers, social workers, dancers, actors, and others—helped respond to student writing. The responders for this course were: Libby Catchings, Diana Dresser, Tara Falk, Nicholle Harris, Reanna Magruder, Joan Dieter Mazaa, Lars Reid, and Joanna Rotkin. Julie Rada, Tess Neel, and Xavier Bird at DU PAI did mountains of behind-the-scenes work to make the course and this anthology possible. Rose Metal Press graciously provided us the book we used in the course, *The Rose Metal Press Field Guide to Writing Flash Nonfiction*, at cost.

DU PAI's pre-pandemic practice was to hold class in person, though this was not possible in late 2020 and early 2021. Necessity, as they say, is the mother of invention. We put together packets of readings and assignments and recorded weekly lectures to DVDs, which were played on CCTV at the facilities. Students did their reading and watched lectures and then completed assignments by hand. Facility staff scanned and uploaded these. Our responders typed out responses, which facility staff printed out and returned to students. Though there were, unsurprisingly, occasional hiccups in this elaborate system (which felt at times like the telephone game many of us played in elementary school), it actually functioned pretty well. It worked well because there were (and are) a lot of people—in CDOC, in DU PAI, friends of DU PAI, and, of course, the incarcerated writers and DU PAI group leaders themselves—who really believed (and believe) that incarcerated people should have access to arts programming. These shared convictions meant that generosity and patience supplied what was needed when our best laid plans fell short. We mention all of this for two reasons. First, it is our feeble effort to sing the unsung efforts of all the people who made this anthology possible. Second, we wanted to explain the intensely collaborative process that, we believe, gives this anthology its unique character.

DU PAI believes that artistic practice, both "inside" and "outside," has therapeutic benefits for the individual and the community. We are also convinced that incarcerated people have important insights and creative expressions to share. The class itself and this anthology were motivated by these two beliefs. One goal of the aforementioned collaboration—and a guiding principle for our responders—was to

2

highlight each writer's unique voice. As you read, notice the diversity of experiences and sensibilities, the variety of styles and technique. Consider the provocative questions and surprising conclusions that these writers offer. Immerse yourself in the range of emotions these pieces explore. We have had such joy in reading and working with these writers and pieces, and it is our great pleasure to share this writing with you.

 —Suzi Q. Smith & Elijah N.

Buena Vista
Correctional Facility

Socks

Is there something magical about socks? Sometimes as I don a pair of socks, I envision my mother. It may sound silly but my mom loves socks. Every birthday and Christmas she will ask for socks. Comfy socks, long socks, colorful socks, fuzzy socks, socks with stuff on them.

I'm afraid to ask exactly how many pairs of socks she actually has. Do they encompass their own closet? There is no way one drawer can contain the plethora that is her cupidity. What does each pair mean to her? Are they destined for specific days of the year?

You would think having socks as one of your favorite gifts to receive would be boring. Her smile upon receipt tells a completely different story. Even though it is a less stimulating present opening experience, she makes it worth it. Bless her heart for leading us on.

I will remain enamored with the memories that a simple sock can conjure. Being away from my mom is arduous but, the reverence of unpretentious stuff helps. The art of using such basic items to continuously bring forth memories of a loved one, is an incredible mechanism of the mind.

The way she lights up on those days, makes the room fill with warmth immediately. The love that can only come from a mom's heart, wraps around you in a tender embrace. The smell of cinnamon and fresh laundry floating through the air. The indelible wonderful feeling of home.

Finding the fantastic in the ordinary is extremely rewarding. Believing in the minor miracles of everyday life can make it bearable. Positive thinking is one of the secrets to navigating the madness. Memories of the past can help us champion the future.

I do believe that socks can be magical. I also believe we can make anything magical. With the right attitude and perspective, life can be just about as special as you want it to be.

MONSEL DUNGEN

I Am

First and foremost, I believe I must explain to you the truths of me, before you dive off into some fantasy of who I might be, only to be shocked and amazed at who and what I truly am. For I am who they say I am.

I look around at painted faces and see smiles that don't belong, and tattooed teardrops that there was no need for. I hear the camouflage of laughter, and listen to war stories told with vigor and excitement—all in an attempt to disguise. I feel like the one in the audience who has paid too much for a front row seat.

You seldom know me as I am, for your society could not stand the burden of my guilt. I am routine where living is a weary task. Many hopeless will perish in my claws, others will go quietly mad. I hold men who hope when hope is futile, who walk my barren halls bearing their burdens quietly with a dignity that shames their captors. Men and women long forgotten by an indifferent world, whose only future is a numbered grave.

I am bitterness in the heart of many who are a part of me, because they were without money or proper friends. I am the contempt of those who have learned that law is not impartial, nor noble, nor idealistic, nor incorrupt, nor simply blind, just dead! I hold the confused and the bewildered whose sin is weakness, and I hold in mass, tired old men who grew up in orphanages, youth authority, graduated to county jail, who have lived under my mantle all of their lives. Nurtured, fed, clothed, washed, worked, entertained and put to bed until they are unable to function outside of my confinement is final evidence of their inadequacy.

There are legions within me, who came from reform schools that reform, but do not teach the zenith of refinement in crime and its glorification. I see acceptance in the dead eyes of those for whom confinement is final evidence of their inadequacy.

Within me are the few who fell prey to passion, who bled and died in your courts, caught in a blind heat, flashing them for an instant back to the caves and now they face the remnants of their lives.

Within me they relive, reform, mutate, cool and distant, waiting for my gates to open. They Will Not Return.

I am more formidable than my high fence, steel doors and gun towers manned by eager twitching faces. I am more terrible than the sum of my parts—or I attack more than the flesh within me, I devour the spirit when I can.

I am prison, I am loneliness and heartache, my teeth sink into the souls of man. I am emptiness and fear, the cold hostile fear that cheapens the sublime spirit of man. I am anxiety that pushes and swells, and uncertainty that smothers and chokes. I am a memory that comes in the night to up and tear and send an anguished cry, only to fade and spring again into a nightmarish scream. I am frustration, futility, despair and indifference. I am all these horrors and more, for I am prison.

I shout my mute contempt for those who govern me and for my lackeys. For they fail to see that through acculturation they become as weak and ill and savage as their charges, but even worse cause they do it for money. I am the face of the heartrending cry of a child in fear of me, in anguish for the loss of his father. I am the monstrous ice cold emptiness and the terror of loneliness in the night of day because, I Am Prison!

GILBERT GONZALEZ

Do I Know?

Day after day I wake up in a place full of men who have made bad choices and mistakes in their lives. Some may wonder, do the mistakes and choices I have made define me? I was told my Father's did. But why? As I sit and think about it, I wonder, what if he was a good man, and Father? What if he was raised in a good home, would he have been there for me? Would he have taught me how to be a man and a Father?

As I am having a cup of coffee, I hear two guys talking about being a new Father. They ask me what I think about being a Father. I stopped and thought . . . I was never taught how to be a Father. My dad was never there for me. The only thing I recall is my Father leaving me.

It is a cool summer day. It is about 62 degrees or so in 1999 at a trailer park in my hometown. You can hear children playing off in the distance. Vehicles starting up, people fighting. I can see it now, my mother standing at the door waiting for me because my dad was late. We pull up in his car. As I grab my bag and start to get out, he grabs my arm and tells me, "I love you son, always."

Thinking about it, I don't see my Father being able to love another person. At that point, a moment of clarity hit me. I asked him, "Are you coming back?" He gave no answer. I wonder what made it so clear to me that I knew he was not coming back. Was it the smell of alcohol on his breath? Maybe the cans of beer in the back seat or the fact that he was a drug addict and an alcoholic. And on the run from the cops. As we sat there I took a mental picture of him. Because only God knows when I will see him again. So when I close my eyes, I can go back to that mental picture, to him. The tattoos on his hands and arms. His long black hair in a ponytail. The lit cigarette in his mouth and a bottle of liquor between his legs.

What's crazy is I realize at that defining moment I didn't want to be like my Father. So with him abandoning me it was time to change my life. I learned to be a man. A good man. A good Father. I guess you can say he did give me the knowledge of what it's like not to have a Father, so I now have the understanding needed to help kids who have or are growing up without a Father.

R Y A N   J .   K R U E G E R

What Hurts the Most

Softly strummed staccato notes. The mournfully melodic moan of a bow pulled across strings. Just a few bars and I'm stopped dead in my tracks every time, paralyzed by the hollow at the center of my chest. After all these years "Going on with you gone still upsets me." The void remains. "I pretend I'm okay." But the emptiness aches even still.

All my days "Getting up, getting dressed, living with this regret." All the lonely years spent yearning. All the hurtful words spoken in anger. All the tears spilled sadly down your cheeks. All the pain perfectly preserved. All avoidable tragedy. All my fault. All nearly too much to bear, "But I'm doing it." All I could ever say, not enough to forgive.

Maybe one day a song won't haunt me, reminding me of the sorrow I've caused. Maybe one day each note won't rend my heart, leaving me to agonize over things I should have done differently. Maybe one day, "If I could do it over, I would trade, give away, all the words that I saved, in my heart, that I left unspoken."

Always I can go back. I need only close my eyes, let the music wash over me, and I'm transported there, to that chill March morning. Head bowed, shoulders slumped, hands clasped behind, defeated. "Being so close," yet unable to hold you. "Having so much to say," but no words. "Watching you walk away," pleading the universe not let it be forever.

Never holding your hand or pulling you close. Never seeing your smile or hearing you laugh. Never kissing you good night, good morning, or just because. Never snuggling on the couch or dancing to our song. Never falling asleep with your head on my chest or waking up and making love. Never growing old together. "Never knowing what could have been," worst of all.

That I loved you long before I admitted it. That I loved you even more for not giving up when things went bad. That loving you brought me back from certain ruin. That loving you was always easy, even when it seemed hard. That I still do, and always will, love you. "That loving you, that's what I was trying to do.

Heart aches, stomach ties in knots, hands tremble, throat tightens, mouth goes dry, eyes burn, tears threaten, whether whispered on the wind or blaring from some speaker, there's no other song that I let myself feel as much. A simple song can be such torture! Did you know it would be so when you sent me the lyrics all those years ago?

Almost everything I ever wanted. Almost all of my dreams come true. Almost a lifetime of love. Almost forever, together, with you. "What Hurts the Most" it's hard to tell. There's not a song long enough to describe this hell. Though if I had to choose, I suppose it would be, the pain I've caused you, not the pain it's caused me.

NICHOLAS LOCASCIO

Half Dead Blue Bic

I grab the half dead blue Bic and now I'm starting, full of fear that once again I'm going to end up abandoning this piece of writing, this piece of me, and relegating it to that abysmal and ever growing pile of strong starts, half decent ideas, and four sentence drafts that litter and pollute the room around me.

I'm apprehensive to begin because I'm uncertain that I'll be able to keep my pen upright and I'm unsure whether my confidence will last as I traverse these narrow and stark white walkways towards an end. But with the half dead blue Bic in my hand I begin taking very meek and tentative steps—word by word—carefully watching and waiting line by line—for the point both in my mind and on the page where there is an opening for me to climb through and run. Watchful for that place where I might be able to break free of the world, and of myself, to sprint and gallivant down and across the page. Watchful for that place, the magic place, where I'm no longer writing, but living. Watchful for that place where my soul can dance freely onto the paper and I'm able to build, with both breath and fire, a space where you, my reader, would want to come and visit. That place is where I want to be. That place is where it all comes easy. That place is where the words are sweet, and golden, and flow smooth from the pen like warm honey.

Thinking back, I can remember when I once lived in that place, the magic place, when the ink flowed freely from left to right down and across the page, when the ink flowed from margin to margin down these narrow and stark white walkways with ease. I don't make it back to that place, the magic place, this time. So it seems that fear I had when starting was well founded because, once again, I am damned to forsake this latest word weaved world into oblivion. With great distress and a heavy heart I begin to slash from margin to margin down and across the page with the half dead blue Bic, shamefully perpetrating another violent vascular vivisection, exsanguinating and execrating the life I had begotten onto the page. Leaving just one more beginning with an untimely end, one more lifeless draft, one more piece of me dead.

WILLIAM PATTERSON

Spur of the Moment

The motorcycle was a custom '95 Yamaha Sec II 720, it was silver with a stinger tail pipe. The day was a hot July summer on a long lonely road surrounded by prairie. The smell of sage, wild juniper, prairie grass and wildflowers mix with the hot asphalt. A speeding silver motorcycle with a young couple on top roar life into the normally silent prairie. An endless of trafficless travel now contains a roaring streak of silver and black. An engine climbing faster and faster is heard followed by the sight of a single headlight of a motorcycle with what could be described as an Ed Ruth poster brought to life. A young man smiling devilishly, his sunglasses glinting in the sun and a young lady gripping white knuckled to his leather jacket. The carefree couple here one moment then gone the next, leaving behind the traces of their speeding moments through time. One could ask as if a member of two birds sitting on a fence, where are they off to in such a hurry? The older of the birds simply states, "Ah! To be young." The prairie is alive with new scents floating across it from its interruption. Cologne, perfume and exhaust. The young man fueled by the adrenaline of his youth as his female companion must reliably trust her safety to him. What thoughts one might wonder are going through their heads, as they speed down the lonely road, what emotions fuel them, what are they sensing?

The road was hot and sticky from the summer sun. The heat of the road kept the tires of the motorcycle glued to the road as if uncounted tiny hands of tar reach up to catch the tires. The pulse of the motor thumps rhythmically in sequence as its R.P.M.s are raised. Man and machine in harmony flowing seamless through time and space.

The bodies of both driver and passenger sway through the wind in a harmonious dance. The hair of the girl flutters behind her head like tiny kites were attached to the long brown strands. The driver's leather jacket crumpled in the grip of his companion as his steady gaze focused on the road ahead. The trill of the speed has the couple smiling in joy. The stinger tailpipe screams danger louder and louder as the speed picks up only to fall on deaf ears of the youth. The vast prairie flushes by in blurs of color and heat. The young man, woman and motorcycle here one moment and gone the next in a spur of the moment. The bird says, "Yes, truly to be young and to believe in the enigma of youth . . . "

Higher Places

If all you had to offer is friendship, like who would still be around? Real situations expose fake people. So sometimes it takes getting down on life to find who's really down. You see, people pretend well when their souls are for sale. Sometimes it's the ones you love the most, that mostly want to see you fail. That's real. Just because they're riding with you, doesn't mean they're riding for you. That's facts. You see, it's more about how they act behind your back. Who can you trust?

Some of us are fighting for people who would throw a punch for us and yet, these are the ones we call friends. You know, the ones that care so much for you about your struggle and yet so silent when you win. The ones that bring gossip to you, about you, but your name, they never defend! Understand everyone in your boat might not be rowing but drilling holes. And as time goes and their jealousy grows, pay attention because that's when true motives get exposed. Everybody in your circle might not be in your corner.

Support doesn't always come from familiar faces. So don't be surprised if God places strangers in your life to take you to higher places. Don't be surprised if your growth makes your circle smaller. But you got two choices, let it break you, or let it make you! Remember it's not the size in your circle, but the loyalty in it!

Whiskey, Switchblade Knives, Pink Mohawks, and a Psych Ward

You know it was goin' ta be bad when, comin' upon the door to your downtown studio apartment, you heard the faint sound of a Maroon 5 song comin' from inside your place. "Fuckin' be alive," you say out loud to yourself as you use your key to open the door. Inside the air is smoky; it looks as if a tornado has crisscrossed its way through your place; and fireball whiskey shooters and CDs intermingle in a large heap on the inexpensive stained carpet in front of the stereo. The speakers are blastin' Adam Levine singin' ". . . And sheee wiill be looved, and sheee wiill be looved." The bathroom light is on but the door is shut. In two quick steps you're jerkin' the door knob and kickin' the bathroom door open—and on the toilet she sits. Alive. Her pink mohawk is all ya can see until she looks up at you with her soft, big brown "doe" eyes that are soaked with tears. Cheap mascara streaks down her cheeks. Ya look ta her cheetah print tattoo'd chest, then down her heavily tattoo'd arms. Cascading from her long elegant fingertips ya notice that familiar sanguinary fluid crashing to the bathroom floor amalgamating with her tear fused mascara. Her switchblade knife rests innocently in the porcelain sink.

Did you know that blood is basic to almost all the body's functions? A blood test can reveal more about your physical condition than almost any other kind of examination. Anemia (a lack of red blood cells) and leukemia (cancer involving a build up of the white blood cells) are just two of the dozens of serious blood diseases. Blood cells are formed in the bone marrow and as such, the bones are an important focus for hematologists.

Hematology, the study of the blood, fascinates me. Hem/hema comes from the Greek word for "blood" and is found at the beginning of many medical terms. Hemoglobin is one, for instance. Hemoglobin is an iron-containing compound found in red blood cells that not only transports oxygen from the lungs to our body's tissues, but then also transports carbon dioxide from those tissues back to the lungs to be expelled out of our body. Coagulation, or thickening of the blood, is particularly important since coagulation is what keeps us from bleeding to death from even a small wound such as a knife cut.

*

Medicated nut cases in the psych ward doing the "Thorazine shuffle" quietly move about aimlessly and mumble to themselves incoherently. "Why are they here? I mean, what's their stories?" You softly say out loud. The expressionless faces don't relinquish any clues whatsoever. Down a corridor ya hear her and her repetitive muffled sounds screamin', "Just let me fuckin' die!" over and over and over, dispelling every lunatic away from that end of the hall. Ya ask yourself "Why are they movin' away from her? What the hell do they know?" Ward staff obviously hear her cries, but do nothin' 'bout it. She's trapped in an unaccommodated room with grey dull walls and left to her own devices to deal with the horrors and demons and monsters her unsound mind is constantly conjuring and in this ward nobody seems to care! Alone and naked, she paces the room as those elegant fingers (and occasional nibble) work to rip out the stitches in her arm and wrist.

M I C H A E L   J .   S I M P S O N

Playground Legend

I can feel the sunshine on my face and the grass between my toes. I hear Tommy yell, "Go deep." I see a vivid blue sky dappled with beautiful clouds as the ball comes into view. All my senses are heightened. I can smell the grass and dirt, feel the beat of my heart and the sweat dripping. I see the ball into my hands and, after a quick spin move, I run down the field. My defender left in the dust. I love my park.

Every day we play for hours on end. Welcome to my childhood. Basketball on nice days, football whenever else, and baseball for a change from time to time. We play and play, these days will never end.

Today is one of those special days with that feeling, our time in the sun will last forever. We play until we tire and take a break on our hill. It's our retreat, a hideout of sorts. The place where innocence is lost. We'll sneak a cigarette and, in later years, a joint. I still to this day feel a certain ownership of that hill. It was my go-to spot for years and years. Anytime I felt sad I seemed to feel better on that hill. It was my fortress of solitude. As we grow, it's less and less time playing ball and more time on as we drink and smoke more. We give up playing ball altogether.

But today we are still into the game. I smell the rain coming and it's time to get to football. Nothing can or will stop us today. We love the game and we will never die.

Buena Vista
Minimum Center

RONALD FRANCIS

Because I Am a Father

The Sins of Our Fathers

Words. Words so vile and ugly, meant to crush a man's spirit and steal his dignity. Words that blacked the user's very soul. Humanity lost.

Nigger, wetback, chink, rag head.

Forced upon us as children. Young and naïve. Seeds of generational hate and intolerance planted and left to take root. Fathers beaming with pride.

We echoed back. Of course we did. Repeating words spoken from the men we looked up to, all too eager to please. Hate and intolerance are learned and we accepted this instruction as Gospel. Words as weapons from the mouths of kids.

The sins of our fathers becoming the sins of their souls.

It was easy to think and say these words when none of us, at the time, had ever really met a person of color. So no harm no foul right? Sticks and stones may break our bones, but words will never hurt us? Not that simple, I'm afraid.

As I got older, I began to question almost everything I was told to believe. I say told to believe because I didn't dare question my elders at the time. Eventually, I could no longer use that as an excuse, and I found it, that is my elders, crumbling all around me.

So, at the age of 47, and with so much more life experience than that stupid young kid, I continue to ask myself why? And when?

When do the sins of a father become the sins of a son?

It is pointless to stop using these words if I continue to water and fertilize the soil where the seed(s) of hate were planted. When you seek the truth, and then find the truth, you cannot then ignore the truth because it is inconvenient or uncomfortable. Three-piece suits and corporate boardrooms do not replace white sheets and backroad cross burnings.

So a choice to be better and do better has to be made. It has to come from within. I hold myself accountable for my thoughts, words, and actions because they have power. To lift up or tear down. It is no longer a matter of color nor any other reason I could think of, so I lift up. Those around me, and my hands in prayer, that we as a country can move forward.

How do we get there? It cannot be by compromise or conformity, by politics or protest, not by tearing down the monuments of our nation's dark and ugly history, without learning first from my own. History exists so we can move toward something greater. So, we must learn from it lest we repeat it.

When I became a father, everything changed. And we have every reason to be hopeful with this generation and those to come. It must be our aim as parents to leave this world a better place for our children and not in spite of our failures. Let them choose love above all else, because we have shown them what love looks like and acts like, equally.

Why does this matter to me? Why do I care? Because I am a father.

And so that the sins of this father do not become the sins of my daughter.

KEVIN L. JAMES

Apprehending Joy

Escaping an ominous storm that loomed under the roof of their home, yeah, that's what they did—they escaped. They absconded into the world in search of shelter. The adults in their lives are volatile, not to be bothered. Apparently, they were too exhausted battling an invisible enemy to rear them without unrestrained violence or constantly escaping themselves. Children left to care for themselves for days or weeks at a time. Abandoned. Kids whose plight was deemed perilous. The world was a different place in 1980. Those boys did not pretend to understand, they flight. Mischievous explorers found in creeks and ditches; back allies and storm tunnels; or anything left deserted. They held a vehement desire to rip off the emotional riot gear worn in the presence of unstable adults. Deliverance that spurred an impassioned sense of adventure. Adventures that engendered a reverential poise over the territory they conquered.

*

Their conquests, though sometimes destructive, did not excuse the malicious nullification of the rights or property of others. They survived in a world unknown to outsiders. Scavengers for food and recognition rarely found within the walls they knew. At times, these boys succumbed to the internal and external taunt, that-in-fact, they were without, by venturing off to steal things beyond what was needed. Not blind adoration nor preoccupation with fickle material things, proof. Proof to themselves more than anyone that they could have anything they wanted. The threat of being swept away by Social Services or in the backseat of a cop car was ever present. To avoid capture, the boys adopted the stealth of Bruce Lee, each move in tandem with shadows, pivoting rhythmically around obstacles, and ducking without error behind the tire of a parked car. Lives imbued by threats and the unrealized treasure of survival.

*

An accumulation of wealth gathered from crawling over broken glass, perched upon battered legs to jostle an old rusty steering wheel, and squinting through the shattered windshield of abandoned vehicles. Though elusive, they apprehended joy and invested countless hours navigating the intricate maze of storm tunnels. The periodic loss of spatial perception and inability to etch out the slightest silhouette did not deter exploration of the darkness. As unsettling as the dark could be, to upset the only angel in life to fill their belly and provide protection frightened them more. The smart, exacting strike, of grandma's hand for repeating a dirty word was devastating. The speed and grip with which she snatched them by the ear, hauled as if they were weightless to the bathroom to wash the filth from their mouth with a bar of soap affected them deeply.

*

Words picked up like the smooth stones at the bottom of the creek bed. The same creek where the boys waded in murky water, splashed carelessly, and engaged in mud wars. They rode giant pieces of Styrofoam miles downstream, oblivious to the dangers that lurked. Adventures, exploring creek shores lined with concrete walls, jagged-jutting rocks, and the thick blanket of marsh beneath ancient trees. Sliding out of control on the slick layer of moss and algae. Jumping blindly off rocks and cliffs. Swinging wildly on ropes tethered high above. Launching their resilient bodies into unknown depths and soft islands of sand and broken glass and hidden boulders. Laughter and tears—stitches and crutches were sure to come. The dirt concealed battered bodies.

The only cleansing achieved. Flood waters were an unpredictable, unannounced, and lingering reality of playing where they did. The certainty that these waters would sweep them away was terrifying and exhilarating. They have confronted and evaded threats for as long as they can remember. The cultured development of acute awareness. Ever alert. Prepared to respond to the inevitable face of danger.

*

These boys do not forsake the life they lived. To relinquish the past would debase the purity of character forged within the crucible of experience. Reminiscent with sober sentiment. To peel back the layers and expose the depth and complexity of suchness requires meticulous unpacking of a priceless gift, life. Each fold uncovers another. Permission granted to glimpse what has shaped them and why they endeavor to absorb the beauty contained in each moment, each breath, and each relationship. As children, they yearned for more than what they saw. As men, they have grown into a mindful regard for what is truly valuable. Tempered by the harsh and often cruel realities of the world. Emergent with an invaluable measure of confidence and the wherewithal to stoically recognize that the road preceding this one did abduct their hope. The interdigitation of an adventurous spirit and imagination allows them to look beyond any obstacles in front of them. As when they reached for the light inside those storm tunnels, this life has confirmed that they do not belong in the dark.

JOHN KLINKER

Free as a Snowflake

Even if you're not a deep thinker or meditator-type, a person can find themselves looking out a window, staring at a snowfall. Rain is special on its own, but snow is very slow in its descent. Catching it in the glow of lights. Looking out at the swirls can be mesmerizing and even therapeutic, allowing ideas and thoughts to formulate.

Late at night, I woke from a dream to see the beauty of the snowfall, dancing in the lights surrounding this Colorado prison. My anxieties of being released into society are minimal, but I'm able to peacefully imagine my responsibilities that ensue. Minds do have a funny way of conjuring up the deep truths of character when forced to react naturally. The body's heart rate dances in faster rhythms than usual when realities of how much I've missed in life come to mind. I personally have been incarcerated for 14 ½ years. Family members have lost trust, gained respect, and reunited within this moment in time of my incarceration. My very own trust and respect for my actions has come into question within myself. However, through trying to look deep within and have an outside perspective of myself, I was able to see where I made mistakes. Some professionals and spectators of my life would say that my ability to find a silver lining in all the sadness I caused is just a coping mechanism. I'd say that through time and reflective thinking, I was able to rise above my faults, recognize the things to stay away from and find forgiveness for myself. The past is done and over by all the standards of time, but the memories of it all still remain. I was 21 years of age when I committed an act of violence that led to death. My time in prison wasn't the norm of fighting, card games, dominoes, tattoos, drugs and wooing women on the phones. Growing up playing sports and being physically active, I clung to my roots. Time did go on and I found myself not balanced with life, so I volunteered for classes and reading. The symmetry came naturally with focus and dedication. Now leaving prison as a 35-year-old man with 91 college credits and a supportive family, I can say that I learned a lot of lessons that got me through struggles within myself and these prison walls. I trust myself to do the right thing for once. Just dancing around . . . envisioning . . . thinking about what it is to be as free as a snowflake . . .

ANTHONY ROSAS

#23

Kids growing up usually have nice rooms. Rooms filled with cool toys to get away. An inviting environment encouraging all the kids who enter to smile. A place where the walls are painted with positive energy colors and don't live by the saying "if these walls could talk." Aromas fill the room constantly, chocolate cookies to be exact. Or they have a tree to escape to where all the boards are intact. Leaves on the tree that are as colorful as a rainbow and full of life. Not me personally, my neighborhood was a war zone, and my getaway was a graveyard. A school bus graveyard that is. School bus #23 was my ghetto version of "The Magic School Bus."

The yellow was so rusted that it looked tan. All the windows except the windshield and the emergency exit were broken. Surprisingly, the seats were in mint condition. It was the vehicle version of myself. If it had a face, it would probably smile when it saw me just as much as I did when I saw it. I felt untouchable and protected. The bus offered safety with nothing in return, but a little T.L.C.!

There was a fire extinguisher that had seen better days that constantly tempted me, but I was way too scared to pull out the pin. My mom was way too busy working countless jobs trying to make ends meet. So this bus was my home away from home, where I was in control of the moment! The radio station was the only real decision, but I seized the moment! I even took a broom to it just in case I ever had company.

That bus was the one place where I truly felt safe. A judgment-free zone. Where I've shedded blood and countless tears upon. I often am reminded of 23 and I wonder if it ever got put back to work. The whole time I thought I was helping it, I now realize it was helping me!

Colorado State
Penitentiary

FRED BARKER

How To Leave Your Sacred Space

You're so silly! There aren't too many people I know who amuse themselves the ways you do when you're alone. You're a trip. Sometimes, it's a song you hear on the radio, or in your head. Other times, it's something you're watching on T.V. that moves you to gushing emotions and your eyes weep so uncontrollably, you're shocked you're crying at all. You be so hyped, chill, and emotional when you're to yourself in that prison cell; I love that about you. I get it; that cell is your sacred space.

By now, you're too old not to know who you are, what you want in life and who you want it with. I know all those answers kind of just crept up on you, but life is funny like that. I also know if you never would've had that time alone, space to "become," you'd be clueless about your identity. But you're searching on how to articulate yourself with others, how to get out of your head so you can mentally, emotionally, and spiritually leave your cell and all the security you've constructed for yourself in there, in order to be "sociable."

It's quite a paradigm to think that your body can be locked up, incarcerated, and yet free in mind, soul, and spirit. You used to loathe administrators and others who would say things like "Just because you're locked up and may never get out, your mind can be free." That statement doesn't capture what it means to lose freedom in order to learn to be oppressed through institutional conditioning. It is true though; you can find yourself so filled of consciousness that to be present anywhere else is unconscionable.

Bruh, you gotta get out of that cell. Step into the wild unknown with confidence and perspective. I got chu, Imma show you how to "step correct" following three basic principles: humility, vulnerability, and chill. Or H.V.C.

There you go again, I see that fixated gaze, pacing the cell. Must've just read something powerful, heard something of wonder, or found your voice in an original thought. Oh, now your lips are curling, what'chu grinnin about: What's her name? Was it Jesus? Was it a quote or saying? C'mon man, say something. Oh, you gone laugh out loud. At times you move like a reed wading on the waters. Peaceful, rhythmic in the wind. See if you can keep up on "how to" leave that peace and go beyond yourself.

First, in order to be at bliss among men of violence and manipulation you must clothe yourself with humility. Humility is a garment of the wise. You locked up too, regardless of how you got here: you here, embrace it. Handle it like zookeepers or wildlife preservationists; be carnal, a natural with beast of the field, a cover for the fowl whose minds are easily persuaded into traps of the waning. For no one is more shunned – whose words and presence carry no weight – than he who thinks himself untouchable. Pride will get you exposed, blood in the water. In the wild, animals know fake, and that can't be you, so stay humble.

You are an aviator, "down" for as long as it takes to get the job done, "grounded" with the purpose to learn what must be learned before making that great celestial journey beyond the grave. What you're learning is how to navigate social spaces. Indeed, life is all about relationships. You're not managing prison; you're managing yourself around and with others. Limitations, confinements, and imprisonments is an issue of stepping out of your own head. At this point, it's not institutional, it's humanitarian.

Oop, you feelin' yourself!! I've seen this dance of yours before, you're at the threshold of unction. You got your finger on the button to open your cell door, but you're not ready yet. You're in such a mode of conflict inwardly about it, you usually accidentally flush the toilet. It's easy to get those buttons confused anyway, don't trip. You pause, you're between who you are spiritually and who you want to be as a servant for others, restrained by who you could be without grace, give yourself more grace at this point.

Finish your thoughts, concentrate them onto that blank page in your journal or your memoir. See, I've witnessed this séance in you many a time, feeling so torn between your rapture of isolation where you can "work" and get some things done, some things out of you and the demands of controlled movement, going out, programs, recreation, library, even shower time. This is where only you can hear the calf-skin drums and smell the incense of spice and myrrh. Your eyes tell your mind's gravity and weight of inspiration, they reveal the orange glow of a controlled bonfire whose embers burn, crackle and roam about your body then hang as ash on the edges of your eye lashes. But what you're feeling in your spirituality is the warmth of the familiar. Thing is, it's also the nakedness of something that often is described as an emotional giant when mastered, but also sends signals to your mind that makes you feel like you're alone. I'm speaking about vulnerability.

Vulnerability is step two to exiting your sacred space. Vulnerability leaves you feeling like nobody gets you; that experience of putting yourself out there, but the love is rarely reciprocated. Vulnerability is a space you've loved to cultivate even though sometimes you feel like you like others more than they actually like you. Stay there, that's your superpower. Feel that weight for other's success, celebrate their victories from your pit of forgottenness. For humility always prompts others better than self, only a vulnerable person can admit this. Vulnerability is your strength.

In order to navigate the social circles around you, you must navigate the unrest within, created *by* you. Get past the "zone" and "mode" of individuality and embrace giving. Giving of your presence to others, giving of your emotional intelligence as much as your intellectual wit when it's in your power to do so. And do it without taking how you're received personally; again, you're getting out of your own head. You may feel like you're giving away your secrets and best self altogether, who you are in private and who you see yourself becoming. But remember, you've shed your best self a hundred times, if not a thousand times, in tears over moments you've lost with loved ones over your penitentiary-bound activities. All smoke, all ashes.

COUNT TIME. COUNT TIME, STANDING FORMAL COUNT!! ID's IN THE WINDOW, LIGHTS ON!

I suppose you realize by now how little in a "prison" is in your control and that your conscious rapture can be shaken from you, but that's why you covet your quiet time so much. Never lose your composure, no matter how unnerved you might get, chill. The last component to stepping out of yourself in order to navigate the maze of what makes people "complicated" is for you to be comfortable with your "chill you." You got moves that you use to keep your wellness well. You've got mechanisms you employ to enter your spiritual utopia. When your ideas of peace and sanity run adrift, go to your identity; never lose your peace out there.

The trick is to be creative with your mind, cautious with your heart, and careful with your chill. You must see yourself as both aviator and air while keeping your commitments and navigating relationships in this concrete jungle. Stay stoic, be easy, chill.

Breaking mental concentration on things important to you is not the end of them, dig deeper. The next time you "gear up" to step up out of that cell, fall into H.V.C. You press and strive to enter that peace as you do in your cell because it's not something that depends on you, it's beyond yourself, that's why it's sacred. That peace, that holy space, get it movin, keep it, share it if you can, cause like Pops told you, "She'll never leave you." That's how you leave your sacred space, you take it with you.

Getting a Home

The day was nothing to write home about. A lot of humdrum, nothing else to fill in the space of time throughout the day. But I can't call it a waste. I was at my desk either immersed in some sort of homework assignment or tinkering around with an origami project. "Highly Suspect," by Lydia, one of my favorite songs to date came transmitting through the radio waves, turning the day into a rollercoaster of emotions. The melody and familiar rhythm takes me back to my 565 square foot dilapidated home on its best day.

On any sane person's initial visual inspection of my home, most would ponder the question, "How is it at all that someone is even living there?" The foundation kicks the house from one side to the other. Front yard is simply dirt! The point is, at one time in its heyday, it was a lovely blue with white trim. After years of the pounding sun and the unforgiving Colorado weather, it certainly had seen better days. The roof sagged further than is mathematically possible, but for some force beyond the realms of comprehension, it still stood strong.

For me and my best bud, Gus, this place is where we called home. Gus, I happened upon by chance after stopping at the animal rescue after a hard day's work finishing concrete. I wanted to volunteer sometime at the shelter but was declined for reasons that, to this day, are unbeknownst to me. But in turn, I was afforded the chance to take a tour of the place. It was orderly and clean. It reminded me of prison, only cleaner. It was kennel after kennel of dogs, some mean and fierce, acting out of either fear or stress. Others seemed depressed with little hope left in their eyes. Others were right at home. The journey through the facility was brief but powerful. The meet and greet that happened by chance, or design, directors in Hollywood could never recreate.

Gus had some unbefitting name placed upon him the day we met. He was out on a walk with an employee of the animal rescue. I was heading out the door on my way to my truck. In the midst of both, well, I got wrapped up in the leash as Gus danced around me, cinching the employee straight into me. The scene brought out the curator with an earnest apology on Gus' behalf, and a laugh out of me that was very much needed. "I'm not sure what got into him, he never . . . " blah, blah, blah. All I could see was Gus speaking to me through his eyes. He held contact with me and when I came in to greet him, he was so gentle and loving.

The following day I found myself coming down the drive again to the rescue, asking would it be alright if I could take Gus for a walk. I had already renamed him before I left the rescue the day before. We got back from our walk and the front desk had already started the paperwork for adoption. They said I had the look in my eye when we met. They knew he was getting a home.

Every morning after that, whether it was an early get-up-and-go-to-work kind of day, or a lazy-sleep-in kind of a Sunday, our routine never faltered much. I'd be tripping over Gus getting out of bed, always close by and right under my feet. I'd let him out to do his business, start the coffee, and turn on the tunes, usually "Highly Suspect" by Lydia, and commence to a Karaoke jam session. The start of our days together.

Home of Heroes

What an honor it must be to receive a Purple Heart, or any other prestigious medal from the military, serving your country. The art of war consists of strategy, courage, strength—a war of attrition if you will. Is this temerity personified? Your name can live through the ages like Hercules and Achilles. More recently Marcus Lutiell, Chris Kyle and Pat Tillman are great examples of American heroes. Commitment to excellence can help push you through the tough times in battle. Your buddies right by your side every step of the way will bring you even closer. Countries have fought each other for many things like freedom, liberty, politics and land. What would it be like to fight Nazi Germany and the Axis powers? Revenge for Pearl Harbor was a notable reason for action and putting yourself in harm's way. The Greatest Generation make us grateful for their sacrifices and should always be honored and respected.

TAM HUYNH

Make It Right

One day I entered the house, my mother was on her way upstairs to my room, and my focus immediately shifted to my mother's movements. Her voice cascaded down the stairs as she called my name. This was the melodious tone of voice that she usually reserved for special occasions, like I was in trouble or when I brought home a bad report card.

When I reached my room, she was standing with her back to me, looking at the walls where pictures of my dream cars were taped haphazardly. When I walked up behind her, I wrapped my arms around her shoulders. I did something. I did something wrong. I had shot two people, and I'm sorry.

My mother turned to face me; tears clung to the corners of her eyes. She pulled me in close to her, embracing me in a warm hug, then inhaled deeply, and looked at me with the saddest eyes I have ever seen. "Are you sorry?"

"Yes."

"Are you going to make it right?"

"Yes, Ma'am."

"Then you go make it right. You go to the police station and you tell the police everything and you face the music. I didn't raise you to shoot anybody. But I did raise you to admit you're wrong. Then you admit what you did to God. He will forgive you, and so will I. I want you to know I will always love you no matter what happens."

I nodded my head to let her know that I understood, but as her words sank in, my heart began to crumble.

You are a young man now, Tam. You need to choose what sort of man you are going to be. You need to choose now. I know you will choose right. I know you will.

I thought about the embarrassment and disappointment that I knew my mother felt over my arrest. I hadn't spoken with her since that night. I felt like I had to deal with the consequences on my own. I had no idea what it meant to be a parent. No idea how it felt to hurt because you knew your child was in trouble. It wasn't until years later that I would learn about the sleepless, tearful nights that my mother endured during the years of my incarceration.

Forever Yours

Her Point of View: I turned up on you like I did 'cause inside I hate life. Stop telling me that I'm beautiful; that's not what I feel like. My mother was addicted to drugs and my dad passed through me in foster homes, every reason for me to be mad. Stop trying to make me happy, I just want to be sad, and keep my feelings to myself. Don't you like it? Pack ya' bags, yelling and screaming at you as you're trying to fix my problems. You're in tears, saying you love me, but my turn up is still heartless. I don't know how to feel loved, and I feel true love don't exist. The only way I'm still breathing is because of this will I built of bricks. I'll turn up on anybody trying to break my wall down. No way I'll let you close enough to hear my heartbeat sound.

The Liquor Bottle: Turned up 'til the last drop. Hope they grab me off the shelf. They always turn up too much with me. They have problems, I'm the help. Turned up in moderation, I could be a lot of fun, but the main ones that turn up with me are the troubled ones. Five shots too many, from in my bottle I see it coming; false sense of courage 'til they so numb, they ain't feeling nothing except for emotions running high. That's when they turn up, turn real. The pain starts leaking out, flowing in the form of tears, or coming out in rage and violence that's been held in for years. Turning up too much with me leads to regrets, a trip to hell, a life of fears. Five shots too many, from in my bottle I see it coming. My turn up intoxicating, so addictive, you're left with nothing. Still searching for the answers for your problems in every drink, for my love, she gives me hate and rejection, the thoughts you think, all it would take is one squeeze, lights out before you blink. Turned up with me, got you convinced this is the only way to think. Lucky for you this time, drank yourself to sleep. I'll be here next time you're down and out.

Forever yours,
"Hennessey"

No Mind

In a culture where instant gratification, stress-induced diseases, war and politics are beamed into our eyes to be absorbed by our minds, and the results appear in our bodies, there is a subject that raises eyebrows and unlocks secret smiles of those who know of it: meditation.

Advertisers invade our living rooms and infect all strata of media with explosive narrations proclaiming "Faster speeds" and "More data." Naturally, we want the better, we desire it, and we seek it out. Supplement commercials prey on our fears of bad health, makeup commercials prey on our insecurity of self-image, and all companies promulgate that their products will set you free, cure you and make you whole. Our credit cards almost teleport into our hands for that soma of relief or trinket of enhancement.

Meditation suplexes the narrative; it is free, it cannot be sold or taken, it does not break, upgrading is free, airport security won't find it, it cannot be outlawed. Where our reality says think more, go faster, stress out, concern yourself, sleep, then repeat, the meditative reality inside allows you to think less, slow down, breathe and exist.

I am by no means a master at meditating. I often get busy, or over-caffeinated which makes meditating like trying to apply eyeliner while skydiving, or trying to sleep in a mosh pit. I get pulled out of meditation by noise or pain. Sometimes I think too much about meditation while trying to meditate, hence the ancient phrase "no mind." Easier said than done, dude in robes. My mind can be a real puppy.

The wonderful thing about the subject of meditation is there is a sumptuous buffet of techniques and schools, origins and teachers patiently waiting to give you keys of your own mind mansion. From Sufi mystics to Zen masters in saffron, there is a flavor and caliber of meditation for every seeker.

My practice is a sampler platter of many traditions barring none, and I am always looking for high performance parts to perfect my technique. The traditions don't guilt you, or scare you with cosmic punishments, no dogma or judgment. It's done by you, for you and enhances your connection to the universe.

Meditation has unlocked an echelon of consciousness I never found anywhere else. It cured me of hypertension, insomnia and stress. It's a shelter, a clinic and a workspace. It's home, it's always there, inside. Meditation is a location where your worries glow away like cherry blossoms, an ocean of peace that washes away the negativity of your day. When life is a car speeding through traffic, meditation is pulling over and lying in a field of flowers, then it's like reaching the eye of life's hurricane; it's like turbulence of life's atmosphere, to reach the still bliss of your mind's zero-worry state, nothing holding you down, the stars of your life shining unobstructed. No matter who you are, your wealth, gender, body type or education, the joy, the elation, the exuberant euphoria of self exploration is waiting. So take the red pill, go down the rabbit hole. Meditation is an adventure that never ends, and just by trying it, you will never be the same.

Kimberly Martin

Normally, when I tell this story, I focus on the fact that I fed my momma in the visiting room. Fed her and gave her a flower and a flowering cactus. I *need* to share our last Christmas, show people the magnificence my momma embodied. I *want* to keep the precious gift she gave *me* that day close. Private.

It's mine.

But this world is wading through the dark waters of plague and presidential tyranny (or piracy . . . political-bent dependant). Countless families are being forced to let their loved ones go from afar—barred by barriers of glass, steel, concrete quarantine. Fathers. Mothers. Lovers. More and more poor pitiful deaths, last hours alone with strange faces blurred behind plastic shields.

Someone needs to read these words. I need to write them.

I asked my mother to give me *her* story December 25th, 2018. As much or as little as she cared . . . dared.

"My story?" She was a little girl again. Hand in hand she led me from the state she was born in to the state she was raised in to the state she died in. Her tiny fingers fluttered against my palm and forgotten dreams found life, reborn for a few feral seconds.

Hey Momma! Pleasure to finally meet you!

In five months, momma, we're gonna have our last visit. You're gonna have your new dentures, at last. I won't tell you that they're too white against your beautiful skin that's now more yellow than golden. I will tell you about a dream I had the night before, where you are sleeping on a stone bench and won't wake up. You'll tell me how you bled out of your backside and woke in a crimson pool. I'll . . . we'll know this will be the last. We won't say it. We'll take a picture. Red coat. White, white teeth.

"I don't feel good, baby." I know you don't, Momma. Cut the visit short. Go straight to the hospital. "OK, baby." But you won't. You're gonna go home. Go to sleep.

When you die, I'll be in the "hole." Solitary. It doesn't matter why. When they come with the clanking chains clanking, binding my feet to my feet, my hands to my hands, to my waist to the phone and I speak to you for the last time, whisper promises that I'm gonna get out of prison. Someday, ooh Child, we'll walk in the rays of a beautiful sun; you'll climb out of the "comfortability" of the drug-induced stupor that's killing you softly to groan because you hear my voice and want to tell me it's O.K. but you can't . . .

When you die, I'll be glad I got your story.

When I cry-write these words, I'll be glad you gave me your story.

Two Sides

One city with two personalities that are further apart than the sun and the moon. Picture a man in the most mundane life of working in a cubicle, only to leave that life behind with renewed energy and vigor of a phoenix from the ashes. The home of my childhood was such a place. Fort Benning and Oakland Park come together to show two sides of the same coin which is Columbus, Georgia.

Devoid of all personality. Uniform and single file is the story of Fort Benning. It's an easy one to tell, but a hard one to understand as to why it's acceptable. The buildings squat, lifeless and painted with color that matches the time they were built, like the hardened war-era old men that live in them. The most imaginative child would have a very hard task of producing any form of fun. Every square mile maximized by being stripped clear of nature for the constant drone of military training and exercises.

Living practically on top of the next family, there was no choice but to co-mingle. It was as if the children were being groomed to fall in line to a pre-ordained life. Not much to do, not much to see: just learn how to be in a cubicle. Day in and day out, learn how to meld with all the unidentifiable faces that pass by. The gloom of this place can be very oppressive at times leading a child to strive for escape. I have to get out of this cubicle.

As if standing up and realizing that there is more to see in the world, my parents discover a place right outside where the cubicle was. This place of joyfulness and sunshine with the stimuli needed, promoting the mindset that it is okay to step out of the ashes of sedated living and stretch your wings becoming that once-dormant phoenix.

The streets are lined with massive trees on either side. Reaching to the sky, towering over the streets, they create a tunnel. Nature everywhere your eyes can look, with houses that each have their own character. Nothing looks alike and the parameters of the mind have been superseded to be active and explore without any regrets. There are open areas to run around and be free. It seemed there was only sun and happy times for all.

The story of Columbus through the lens of a child may very well be different as age and maturity take hold. Both sides of the coin come together to tell one place's story and as the coin is deciphered the walls of the complacent and boring fall away for the light of proactivity and individualism to enter. So very different from one another, but each needed to be whole . . . the two sides of one city so now that everyone can know it as I do.

MARIO RAXON

My Bad

In the ragged hours of the night, when the cold and rain are paralyzing, he staggered from the darkness. The soft warmth of his brother's home was inviting. The lights were dim and he was aware of the sticky sweet aroma of kettle corn mixing with the burning of candles and an earthy sage incense.

In the upstairs bedroom he'd sat in a greenish bean bag, bedraggled with his dirty tan hoodie, his waterlogged dreadlocks and a soaked black duffle bag overloaded with guns.

His brother untroubled and stoic sat at a desk playing a video game on a computer. The light from the screen played off posters of *Fear and Loathing in Las Vegas* and dead rock stars. His brother's face was aglow: red, gold, green, red again.

The black bag had grown heavy in his arms; the chemicals were dissipating from his bloodstream. His body sagged, his eyes fluttered and his head had hung. He'd asked a question, his words were indistinct. His brother had responded "What?"

"Would you like to buy a gun?" he asked again,

"No," his brother had replied, and with a look of compassion, had covered him in a blanket.

His eyes had glossed, again fluttered and then closed. In his dreams he had been in a blaze. He was no longer in his tan hoodie covered in dirt and soot. He stood calcified, a frozen tree, petrified in a forest that had been engulfed in panicked wildfire. His limbs felt phantom, rooted and simultaneously semi-present. The flames fulminated, thunder and light . . . uprooted, the explosion pushed him back and down as smoke and powder from the chemicals had choked him. Choked him 'til his tears had flown free. He had been a deer in headlights, a frozen tree framed by light and fire.

Plucked from the ground he was dragged to his feet, the black duffle shoved into his hands. Propelled from the house a soft voice had spoken to him. "Hold onto this. It's all I have. I'll be right back." The voice was steady. The voice was Bryan.

He awakened, he was aware. His brother, standing over him holding Eggo waffles, asked if he was hungry. He'd replied "No." His brother had examined his appearance in the illumination of the morning light and commented on his disheveled and soiled state.

"What's this stuff on you? Dirt? Soot?" his brother inquired.

"I don't know," he replied.

His brother studied him quizzically as he continued. "I saw on the news that a few blocks over a meth lab torched a home." His brother's eyes narrowed. "A guy inside was burned alive, in front of his neighbors. He couldn't get out of an upstairs window."

Immobile he had sat staring, the image of a frozen tree illuminated by wildfire. His trance interrupted by a familiar voice. "Bro. Why are you dirty as fuck?" his brother demanded. "You're getting . . . soot all over my bean bag."

"My bad," was all he had been able to say.

ROBERT RAY

Ordinary Object

It was close to noon when he placed his priceless on-the-brink-of-extinction tablet into my dependable hands. With both palms up, I carefully secured his possession with a gentle grip, then cradled it like a proud dad would do his newborn child. I look down at its shiny, black, tranquil glass face and catch a sight of my overjoyed reflection, smiling back at me. Hmm, its happy to see me as well.

Once I confine myself inside my cell, I focus on mentally transforming my concrete dungeon into my cozy oasis. I begin by placing my fingers on the heart of this brilliant device. I press down, with the exact amount of pressure needed, on the button and watch as life surges throughout its body. My excitement grows faster than a crowd on Black Friday the moment I see it's alive. My fingers enthusiastically tap the screen, pin-pointing the music app. They want to be in as if they had minds of their own. It's been a while since I've had some "me" time with my biggest luxury, so I decide to allow it to decide what it wants to say to me, by pressing play, then random: Rick Ross's "Sixteen," Beanie Segal's "What Ya Life Like," and Jay-Z's "Song Cry" reach out of the speakers and caress my soul and emotions.

As of right now, the gadget I once cradled like an infant is an infant no more. It has morphed into a dragon that I am able to vibe and have fire conversations with. I am talking about conversations I can dance to. Dialogue I can laugh at. And even heart-to-hearts that evoke memories that were so forgotten, I shed tears the instant they materialize.

Caught in Time

Pencil in hand, you look and see
An image, framed. Caught in time
A ballerina stopped en pointe
You see beauty, her grace, art
Shared now and passed along.
Inspired, you take your place in line,
Her beauty alone could be your muse.
But those lines, her strength, her grace,
This pose, caught, framed by someone's eye,
Shade, shadow the dance of light.
An image of, can be rendered by hand.
But how do you dream her emotion, capture the joy?
You know what you see, but there is more.
We see what we see, but what do we not?
Her hours of practice, passion, her sacrifice,
Movement from music, that is something else.
Composed, performed, meant for the dance.
She becomes the music, the story choreographed.

The dialogue of art is sensory. You must hear. You must see. But to feel you must experience the emotion, the joy, the love. You can render—draw what you see. But to draw the music she hears, the story being told, you need more than just that flash of time. All that she performed leading to that moment has passed, a memory to her and to who witnessed it. A flash in time only known to you in this image.

Reference to draw, yet for you to honor it, you must express with the same love her art. Now yours, the beauty is the same.

LARRY THOMPSON

Sublime: An Homage to the *Shawshank* Oak

The season of transition was upon them . . . She watched and waited as so many of her loved ones drifted away. Peering down through the clusters that remained she whispered from on high, "Just look at him sitting there; that peaceful, quiet smile spread across his glowingly dark face as he holds the treasure which he found beneath that glassy black rock that looks as though it doesn't belong. He seems content, as though he knows exactly where he's going. I wonder, where will he become settled and rooted?" Restlessly her companions softly murmured, "Wherever the wind blows, that's where he'll be found. Wherever the winds blow."

After a moment of reflection she quietly replied, "Just for a moment, imagine that you're free—without reservation or remorse, free just to be whatever you want to be." And then she waited some more.

In the warmth of the autumn sun, the ol' oak trembled then gently spoke, "Creations of Father God and children of Mother Earth...how marvelous are we? Neither vain nor unsightly, we are beautiful, not insignificant. Beautiful simply because *we are necessary*. What will become of them without us?" When she received no reply, she continued in a singsong manner as though lulling her babies to sleep . . .

"Never shall we stray far from where we've begun and glorious is the journey as our fates are surrendered unto the waves of destiny. With a multitude of shapes and the brilliance of hue, your luminescence is best appreciated when through an unfiltered lens it's viewed. Less nimble than fearless feathers which are suddenly lost in flight, you'll dance and silently celebrate while descending into the dark of a long winter's night.

Oh, to know the embrace of untrampled blades of grass, or the sensuously sweet scent and the velvety soft touch of a speckled white honeysuckle rose . . . The strength of the golden wheat's stalk as it bows before the wind without losing its purpose or sense of identity, and the magnificence of the sunflower as it lifts it's heavy head to follow the path of the bright morning star all the day long, come rain or shine. How marvelous they are—marvelous indeed. Such faithfulness is to be praised. Without Us, what will become of them? For we are the harbingers of photosynthesis and your short lives do in fact matter. You are leaves rustling in the breeze; you are meaningful, and your beauty is . . . "

Suddenly set free, totally disconnected from the only life she'd ever known, slowly she floated down and quietly landed in the faded blue tin box. Redd noticed the addition and fondly reminisced about his friend's easy and graceful stride. Picking her up, he held her under his nose and deeply inhaled the freshness of her freedom and the relevance of her essence . . . Carefully he slipped her into the envelope with Andy's letter. After wiping his brow he put the envelope into the box, stood, then looked skyward and basked in the full glory of the tree which had been the tin's sentinel for so long . . . Softly he wept for joy. Pressing his fingers to his lips and then to her gnarly trunk he paid homage to the great white oak leaving an invisible, yet indelible mark of gratitude, knowing with a soulful pang that he'd never see Her again. Collecting his jacket, hat and the tiny tin box he said goodbye and gracefully backed away.

Stepping out from her shadow and into the amber glow of the early evening sun, with that peaceful quiet smile upon his aged and weathered dark face, he thought while looking towards tomorrow, "I'm so happy and blessed to have met You, my friend—truly you are . . . *Sublime.*"

Colorado Territorial
Correctional Facility

Forces of Nature

Nothing shapes our lives more forcefully than suffering and love.

Pumping through my headphone's wires, D'Angelo's "Brown Sugar" album was injected into my ear canal like an antibiotic sent to cure the poverty that infected my childhood. The world seemed a jumbled mess of happenings—a whirlwind of bad decisions driven by sadness and addiction—that led me here, to the floor of my grandmother's formal living room in the new cramped quarters of her humble, single-story home. Where I slept.

The pristine carpet, covering the house's foundation like a fresh, midnight snowfall atop a suburban driveway, was decades old. From down here in my makeshift bed, I could even see the still-shiny, synthetic fibers shimmering in the moonlight. This room, adorned with her most cherished furnishings, was normally off limits. It represented a lifetime of my grandmother's sedulity and sacrifice, and here I was tramping all over her accomplishments like a child at play in the winter weather.

As naïve and unsophisticated as I was at fourteen, I fully understood why I had a cement slab for a mattress. The spare bedroom was shared by my two sisters and being a male in my family meant toughness was expected. I took on the challenge without complaint viewing it as an opportunity to impress my father. I learned, over those years, the truth about gravity— the truth of how the Earth's mass forces us down toward its center—and as I laid on my side on that unforgiving surface, I could feel the entire weight of the world pressing down on my shoulders. Those years hardened my mind in a way only possible through suffering.

So, on my back I laid (another lesson quickly learned), eyes closed, longing for a normal life. My Walkman spun the magnetic tape inside the cassette from reel to reel, flowing through the first song, into the void of recorded silence. A moment passed, then the second song—the story of my young life—smoothly streamed into my consciousness, tickling my temporal lobe. And that night I heard "Jones in My Bones" for the very first time.

I was floored.

A medley of rhythm and blues, hip-hop, jazz, and soul, D'Angelo has crafted a masterpiece, and this song—this album—told me who I was. Somehow, through nearly unintelligible vocals this song has the words my innocent heart was too inarticulate to express. The lyrics: "What I wouldn't do to get next to the things that are meant for me . . . " became my gospel.

It was once said, "A great song will either make you look upward or inward," and D'Angelo took the cacophonous predicament I found myself in and harmonized it, creating a melody that transported me to a place of self-discovery. I soon realized, I was there, sleeping on that floor, not because we were poor, but because I was loved. My father and grandmother did what was necessary to keep our family together, and that song—those five minutes and fifty-six seconds—helped me make sense of the humanness of the world. Those few minutes softened my heart in a way only possible through love.

B R A D L E Y   E R I C K S O N

Table for One

He collected the bones of the young. Then rough-cut carrots, onions and celery. Mirepoix (meer-pwah). Splitting the mirepoix and veal bones evenly between two sheet pans. He painted and slathered the jumble with tomato paste. Into the box at 400 degrees. Tanned with a pseudo-Bahamian glow, air tinged with acids from the paste. Out of the box and into the pot. A magical brew! Sheet pans caked and burnt. One man's garbage, this is the treat! Empty, yet full of flavor, the pans go back into the box. He uncorks a bottle of red. Nothing proper about this presentation.

The pans began to stir. Screaming, popping, sizzling, and contorting like the witch Gretel tricked into the oven. Out of the sweat box and thirsty for a drink, he generously doused the pans with red wine and angered its spirit. Violently hissing the flavor releases from the pan. Deglazing. Scraping the goodies into the brew and to the top with water. Low heat for the overnight.

The next day's aromatics communicate the arrival of Demi reduced by half. He babied his French mother sauce by straining it through a China cap. Cooling it quickly. Demi-glaze (demi-glaze).

Pulling his dry-aged angus tenderloin out for the butcher. Carefully removing the fat and silver skin, greedily saving the center cut for himself. Salt, pepper, wrapped in bacon, covered in plastic, and displayed in the cooler marveling its marble.

He greased his pan with butter. Added a flour finger handful of fresh minced garlic. His Yukon potatoes so thin that they rolled off the razor-sharp edge, into golden scrolls. Spreading them evenly. Heavy cream, enough to keep the starch gasping for air, two, three finger pinches of kosher salt. Stripped naked, one twig of fresh rosemary. Dressed with a layer of thinly sliced smoked gouda, covered with tin foil and into the box at 350 degrees.

He prepares his marinade starting with fresh minced garlic, balsamic vinegar, extra virgin olive oil, salt and white pepper. He collects and cleans his vegetables, discriminating zucchini from squash, cutting them both on a bias and the red pepper into rings. The dinner bell! It's called mise en place (meez-on-plahss) "Everything put in place".

Like clockwork, the earth shook. People running everywhere. Walls struggled to contain the noise. Dishes clacked and silver chimed. In the weeds where he thrives until . . . They are gone. He cooks for himself while cleaning. Places his filet on the grill, along with his vegetables. Into the salamander with his potatoes.

His hard work culminates to the instant he is alone. The plate is done, minus all the fancy garnish. The roar of the fireplace drowns out the dead silence. Alone at table ten.

The feature: an applewood smoked bacon wrapped filet mignon served over top of a wonderful honey demi-glaze. Alongside fresh rosemary, garlic, scalloped Yukon gold potatoes, finished with smoked gouda cheese and grilled Mediterranean vegetable medley. For dessert, he collected himself for a piece of quiet.

NATE FISCHER

Something in the Air

The Bering Sea air in winter is like a polar bear awoken from its winter slumber too early: cranky, violent, cold, hungry and could easily be the death of you or me if we are not careful. Each blast of arctic air is salty and wet and compels you to seek out shelter. "How much of my icy breath can you take?" it asks.

In Washington, the Puget Sound slices deep into the land. It brings with it a calm and comfortable feeling—peaceful. It is salty, fishy and moist but calm like an old lady in a rocking chair—someone you would like to get to know.

Dry, restless and ravenous, each gust of desert air seeks to take from you all it can. It is a wild animal lost and lonely, starving and desperate. If you remain too long, it will consume you or you will become what it is.

The San Juan Mountains are full of life and growth. Each breath fills you with vibrant, healthy life. It fills your whole body like you didn't know was possible. How could a breath feel so amazing? This must be how a glass being filled with cold, clear, clean water feels.

Wet, heavy, green, the air of Illinois lays on me like an old wet blanket. It seems I carry it around all day, my lungs and skin are running a marathon. The rot, decay, and growth all compete for supremacy in my nose. It is the sweet smell of honeysuckle that wins the day.

ROBERT D. GANDY

The Ride

The balloon was taller than I had imagined, yet only partially inflated, rising what appeared to be more than fifty feet into the air. Not a circle, more egged-shaped, the orb was a patchwork of colors, noticeable from afar due to its hues of oranges, reds, and blues, hovering on a grassy bank of the reservoir. At that very moment, I hadn't known the odds were against me, being here to experience this.

Hours before the scheduled lift-off, alone on a moss-covered boulder at the edge of a wooded plot of land, I was surrounded by towering trees, their colors masked by darkness. The odor of damp earth from the morning dew, and the smells of unseen evergreen and aspen trees caressed my nostrils. My ears sensed, rather than heard, the night-time denizens of the forest scurrying not far away. The snap of a twig nearby announcing something larger than a common field mouse or other nighttime creature ending its nocturnal foray. The leaves of invisible trees bristling as they awaken in preparation of the coming dawn.

I was losing the battle occurring only in my head, not conscious of how nature awakened from its nightly slumber. Some time ago, I had abandoned my friend Ezra Brooks, or maybe, the charcoal-browned whiskey had abandoned me. No answers had been found in that bottle. We both had acknowledged that I was running, the unanswered question remained, (who was asking, anyway?), was I running "to" or running "from"? One way or the other, the answer would be revealed with the unstoppable rising of the life-giving star.

Stillness. There is a calm, a peacefulness, in those few precious heartbeats between when the twinkling stars go dim, and the egg-yolk disk peaks over the horizon, like a bygone burlesque showgirl teasing you with what might be. If you wear a watch, or even glance at a clock, you are sure to miss it, but the vastness of everything: birth, life, loss, death, everything is apparent for all to absorb in those brief breaths of time between.

The Eldo was old only in its years. Recently restored to show-room condition, a gift to myself. Eggshell white exterior; baby blue leather interior. A massive piece of automotive technology. Built as a status symbol for its era. Seventeen feet long, iron and steel, not easily replicated plastic, of today's conveyances, considered a "collector car." For me, the Cadillac was for comfortable cross-country escapades . . . or escapes.

An electric blue colon was flashing the passing of the seconds on the digital clock in the behemoth's dashboard, an unneeded staccato reminder that the eastern sky was becoming more illuminated. I perceived my fingers gripping too tightly on the supple, leather-wrapped steering wheel. I glance at the neon white needle of the speedometer, my mind barely registering that it is flickering like an up-tempo metronome, between 110 and 120. Too fast for the speed limit; not fast enough to reach my destiny. It's all indistinct, nothing but fuzzy shapes whiz by. The future of the world—my world—is dependent on whether the Gods, Fate, Mother/Father Nature, show me favor in the next nanoseconds. It's too late for me to own up and be responsible. I have no reasons, only poor excuses.

The numbers on the dashboard clock yell at me, screaming, "YOU'RE LATE!!!" I don't know if they will still be at the rendezvous location, the parking lot of The Fort, a few acres of pavement in the middle of nowhere for one of the best steakhouses in town. There is still room under my right foot, but this chariot of luxury is built for comfort, not speed. Without thought, foot and floorboard become one.

Tires screeching, trying to maintain grip and the Eldo turns and enters the parking lot. The small group has been waiting almost an hour and were now getting back into their cars. I almost honked my horn but my sudden, and reckless, appearance has been duly noted. Nine people assembled, family and guests. The youngest, our six-year-old daughter, the eldest, her 66-year-old grandmother. Each of the nine loved by at least one other person in attendance.

My appearance at this moment has brought tears to some, possibly tears of happiness. At least one of the assembled was not overly happy with my presence at this particular time. Only later did I discover that there had been a betting pool, squares on paper, on whether I would be late, or even show up at all.

Afterward, a caravan of four vehicles traversed to Horsetooth Reservoir where the pilot and ground crew were inflating the balloon, awaiting this motley crew of first-time passengers. This was no ordinary pleasure flight. The pilot and uniter, patiently waiting for this over-dressed-for-a-Thursday group.

As the wicker basket skimmed over the placid waters of the reservoir, a right of a passage for ballooners, Carol, my mother-in-law as of ten minutes ago, whispered in my ear, "You are wonderful, and I won the pool!"

DARNELL HINKLE

Transformative Times?

Hyper-sexed, drug-infested, social-racial discord and the pseudo-individual 1960's were not what they seemed. And 2000-to-present, our society has been inundated from within by fear and every level of dehumanization, to include guilt and fear. "Oh, go shopping and carry-on with your day" . . . No worry. Is this possible? What do you think?

All things considered, the transformative 1960's, in large part, passed over me and my family. That time was not a preview of our future. Indeed, my family "broke" in several ways, several times. A sense of safety and good will existed only from within, sometimes. So, I held my nose up and studied like never before and only thought of myself and quickly rejected others before they could reject me and that imaginary control gave a false sense of security.

I think our reactions and reality are what we feed them, what we hold dear, right or wrong. I imagine the '60's as uncertain, malevolent, disgusting as identical as the 2000's in an environment of anxiety, anger, guilt, shame, people calling for anarchy, supporting racism, and superiority . . .

Now is not the time to go shopping!

Words

Words have a power seldom seen elsewhere in this world. They have the ability to inspire legions of devotees, shape human life and write history—in both the sense of documenting and creating it.

Communication is certainly one of the key aspects of humanity. Did our advanced evolution provide us with the means to transmit and receive ideas more effectively, or was it our skills at communicating that drove our evolutionary process far beyond that of any other creature on this planet?

Either way, words have become a vital part of us. The lyrics that brighten our day. The digital characters sent over the internet that allow commerce to thrive. The quiet conversations between those whose lives are interwoven.

And yet, how often are words insufficient, meaningless?

How could something as trivial as words describe the joy of experiencing new life being brought into the world? Or the ache of what one knows will be the last time talking with a loved one? Or the inescapable solitude of realizing how fragile this short life is?

Such feelings are utterly unexplainable, indecipherable, but nonetheless real. The question then, is how to express this. How to upgrade the dimensionality of language to reflect the higher order of reality. If the intricate statues of the human experience cannot be chiseled out with mere words, can these tools, if wielded skillfully enough, at the least carve a detailed relief depicting such scenes?

Perhaps, it is not the words themselves that contain power, but rather the craft of connecting them in meaningful arrangements where one begins to create, to inspire, to wield a force as compelling as any found in nature. By choosing the right words, omitting the needless ones, and stringing them together accordingly, one can transcend beyond quantifiable communication through verbal or written methods to express the underlying and overarching themes that shape us all.

Everyone can strive for this—to tell stories that matter.

JEFFERSON KISER

More Than a Label

The human race seems to have an innate need to categorize and label everything and everyone. Perhaps this is because of some desire to identify where we fit in the universe. To be sure, people in prison have been labeled in more ways than it is possible to count. What is often overlooked is that these labels describe what we are, or have been, but they do not necessarily define who we are. There are some who demonstrate every day that the labels with which one has been branded have nothing to do with who they can actually be.

Because this prison has been designated a medical facility, there are a significant number of its inmates who, for a sundry of reasons, have been betrayed by both time and body. They are those sufferers of disease, and/or advanced age, who have been forgotten by society, left to do nothing more than await death. For lack of a better term, we will call these men patients.

The presence of these patients means that there also exists here a handful of men who defy all logic concerning being an inmate at a correctional facility. They display a level of altruism that is rare outside the walls of incarceration, and nearly unheard of inside them. They are those uncommon and amazing men who, in a multitude of ways, truly bring care to those amongst us who are unable to care for themselves. These caregivers are benevolent. Valkyries who help deliver those disregarded souls through the final and loneliest days of their lives, into the next existence, with as much comfort, dignity, peace, and even joy as can be gathered in such a purgatorial environment as this. These men exemplify what it means to not let what we are define who we are.

The select Offender Care Aids (OCAs) who tend to the daily needs of these patients single handedly take on at least a portion of the roles of what would be no less than half a dozen different people for someone being treated outside of prison for the same diseases. CNA, physical therapist, nurse, caregiver, counselor, and family member are all titles that could be held within the scope of the daily duties of these men. These OCAs help patients deal with the pain, frustration, anger, fear, humiliation, and inconvenience experienced by anyone suffering from such horrible diseases as lupus, ALS, and cancer. They do all of this, every single day, without losing sight of the fact that underneath it all, they aren't just taking care of another prisoner, they are taking care of a fellow human being.

What develops into the greatest difficulty for these OCAs is *not* that they become detached from, or callous to their job, but that they become involved with every patient as an individual person. They are *present*. They grieve where no other people are available to share in what should be a profound family experience, continuously taking part in an intensity of emotion that most people will feel only a few times in their entire lives. Watching this happen over and over again may seem like a curse, but they will tell you that, ultimately, it isn't about them. It is about caring where no others dare to care, and the transcendence involved in giving that care. The fact that they wear the label "inmate" has been rendered completely irrelevant. They have taken all that their job requires and molded it into a label that is truly noble. If only we could all, in our greatest time of need, be blessed with the help of someone as gracious as these men who have redefined the label, OCA.

By virtue of being incarcerated, every prisoner will forever carry a laundry list of negative labels. However, by not being concerned about the labels that have been placed upon them, and simply giving the best of themselves to those whose time in prison, and on Earth, is simultaneously coming to an end, these purveyors of succor have been made caring far more important than labels. It is in this that these tenders of an ailing man's trip into that final light, in this place of so many things dreadful, have elevated another label to mean something exponentially greater. Inmate or not, they might just be a little better at being human than the rest of us.

DAVID LARKIN

Wild Places

It had been two years. We had to move when my dad lost his job as a pastor. It was no secret he had been beating my mother for years. I guess there was some kind of warped small-town code that made it okay. Until he left the marks on her face anyway. A five-fingered shape that didn't start to fade for days. That's how we ended up in Vegas living in a house that was sometimes filled with fighting and screaming. But mostly it was just that deep malicious silence clinging to the walls.

I was ten when I signed up for a hiking club. And only because once a month I would be gone all day on a Saturday. I don't remember anyone from the club, not anymore. But that first trail experience changed me forever.

We drove four hours to get up into the mountains where trees could grow. An actual forest, I had never seen anything like it. And it smelled just like Christmas! The air was cleaner and the sky bluer than I thought possible. Such quiet—not silence—but the quiet of peace. Bristlecone pines were whispering their secrets to one another. A creek, murmuring something. I couldn't make out any words, but I felt almost like it was saying something I should try to understand. The great taciturn stones were listening to it all. Ageless with nothing to say concerning that countless millennia they have witnessed. I had been to church, but it was an actual spiritual experience.

This trail, nothing more than a dirt path, led me through an entirely new world. The meadow that provided hints of deer, our teachers pointing out the evidence. The grasses gathered near, swaying all together in the trance of an afternoon breeze. Water in the brook giggling with anticipation then breaking into laughter at the little waterfall. A ridge giving way to unexpected, beautiful views. How could a dirt path take me to such wild places? It was on this trail I suddenly felt safe, whole. Somehow able to take a complete breath. Free from the insanity, that until this moment, I believed permeated all the world. Able to just—*be*—in this place.

I walked that path; brought back no talisman, no treasure, such as children often do. No fallen leaf or random stone. But came back changed, compelled to return to wild places over and again. To breathe clean air under a blue sky. To stand in the trance of an afternoon breeze. To laugh with the water and sit listening to the secrets of the trees. To renew myself and be reminded, insanity is not everywhere.

ANDREW MCCLAY

You Find Yourself

When that cell door slams shut for the very first time, and you find yourself alone and cold and frightened, that is when your former life is severed and you are left in ruins. You stagger to the mirror that is like you—broken and bent and beaten—and you see someone you barely recognize looking back at you and you ask "How?" and "Why?" and "What the fuck have you done?" That's rock bottom. That's when you know nothing is ever going to be the same again. That's when you're at the crossroads when you wish you were dead and you feel like dying and you think you deserve to die, but you're alive. Whether you deserve it or not, you're still alive. You still have to breathe.

You see, life is always what you make it. Whether you're in good health or bad, or you're rich or you're poor, or you're free or in prison, the responsibility is squarely on your shoulders. You make the decisions every day, and you choose to live a responsible and happy life in which there is meaning and purpose, or you choose to be a weak and miserable wretch who is too busy feeling sorry for themselves to take charge of life and actually live your days rather than just survive them.

When that cell door slams for the very last time and you've done the hard work to ensure that you are a good and decent and respectable person, then you have found redemption. You've picked yourself up and owned your story and taken accountability for the worst thing you've ever done without letting it define you. You've made the right choices day after day and year after year to have become a person of integrity and character and living a life in which you never hurt anyone again through your bad decisions and careless actions. You will have lived your life to be someone who is truly worth finding.

TIMOTHY WAKEFIELD

How to Smile: 101

Nurture me with the gleaming immaculate tools you use to chew your food! Squeeze the consternation of a hard day out of your face by flexing your all-powerful muscle, zygomaticus major. Exaggerate the wrinkles of time around the eye's corner where tears flow through tiny tributaries to laughter from jokes told and the happiness you experience witnessing a new born baby yawn for the first time. Smile: the most sacred meditation. It is what makes you you and impossibly anyone else. You may not be able to duplicate anyone's, but you may have to steal some when others are not looking. The smile can even tell twins apart. Go ahead, try it in the mirror. Feel your own face changing form in the deepest reaches. Notice what happens where the formless resides. Maybe your heart flutters, diaphragm turns into a smile of its own as you breathe. Deeply! Oscillate between frown and smile. You're standing before yourself. You can change the world or just brighten the day. Just . . . by shifting your cheeks and lips. There's a lot riding on the zygomatic arch, but this is no ordinary roller coaster. It's your cheek bone and it is more fun, and takes less energy than frowning. Relax! Stretch your lips like curtains revealing a stage. Radio City Music Hall! Reveal your teeth, pearly white or yellow, crooked or straight, they'll glisten . . . in unison. The dancing performance of your joy. Unless you are smiling behind my back. An acknowledgement of my folly in a way that says, "I told you so," with the flash of a smirk. The kind of half smile that causes one's ears to slide backward, one eye squint and the opposite eyebrow to lift the forehead into crinkles that might say,

"I hope you didn't mean to do that."

The most critical step to smiling comes when your head meets the pillow for the nightly rendezvous. Close your eyes. Smile like it is your career and you get paid on commission while thinking of me because smiles to me are returned duty free.

Denver Reception and Diagnostic Center

STEVE ALLEN

The Elusiveness of Beauty

Beauty like time is elusive and fleeting. We seek to find it and then to capture it. Yet it always slips away. Time takes its toll, no matter the care. We can sometimes slow it down, but we can't save the day.

The shiny new truck, the brand-new bike, glistening like jewels in the flashing Christmas lights. The memory, the joy, of a wish came true. Each day that passes slowly dulls the luster and shine. Time takes its toll, and the payment comes due.

The family photo album becomes a time capsule. A futile attempt, to capture each moment, clipped on pages, of a dusty old book. Time takes its toll, and the memories slowly fade. We gather round the table, just to take another look.

Memories and collectables, just snapshots of the times. We found the elusive grail and beauty caught our eye. We will keep on searching, there's so much more to find. We share the stories, we tell the tales, and encourage others on their guests. For even though, time takes its toll, every moment of beauty, is well worth the grind.

Although beauty may be hard to find and all too often fades away. It's the hunt for those elusive treasures that keeps us in the race. We must push on and seize the day. For the goal is just a part, it's often the stops along the way, the thrill is in the chase.

Elusive or not, beauty is all around us, and time can be our friend. Value every moment, appreciate the time we have. See the beauty in creation, and capture it when we can.

TRAVIS BARNES

NOW: Of Time and Eternity

I have this idea about time. The first thought you'll need to follow in my line of thinking is this: You cannot "NOW" because "NOW" never leaves, and wherever you go, and whatever you do, "NOW" is always with you, even in your grave . . . or prison cell.

To prisoners, time seems to be against us, because it is in time, yes, it is in the minutes and the moments that we have placed both our hopes and our dreams. As time continues to march on, our hopes are then strangled by despair, and our dreams then become the very monsters of our nightmares. It is a strange observation perhaps, but you really don't notice "time" until you are standing before a judge that has sentenced you to "serve time." Naturally, "time" is all around us; it is attached to you and me. In the simplest of equations, you and I (as human beings), are in essence "energy moving through space."

Time is relative to space; it is the measure we use to track energy's movement through space. Everything we "do" takes "time" to get "done." So, we press on through time, with our time as if we are time; yet, we feel like we are behind the "times" all of the "time"! We are the time machines of men's dreams, always forward never back; and yet, ever the "NOW" and never onward! Everywhere we are not is "there," everywhere we are is "here," vainly aiming to move beyond this space in time to a place in time outside of the confines of this journeyless journey.

Like "time," we prisoners are invisible. Always moving yet always in the same place. We are now the seconds, we are now the minutes, we have become as hours, and days, and weeks, and years! Yes, we are calendars and clocks, made of all the things that when we are looked at are forgotten. He was a baker, she was a lawyer, I was . . . the wood on that clock that was a tree, the paper of the calendar was too, the leather on this watch came from . . . forgotten things, lost in "time"; yet still here and "NOW." Can you see it? "Now" is all the "time" we will ever have. Sure, you can be aware of the "times" and "seasons," but we are all of us trapped in the presence of the present! So where is eternity!?

PAUL FREEMAN

Passing On

Through the many different ways of love, learning lessons in life we can feel and see how our loved ones in our lives have passed down to us . . . the fine joys of happiness. The thoughts of our loved one whose journey in life to the next, plays its part in our lives we live now. A look in the mirror, a taste of our own cooking, a loving lesson passed down to a next family member as generation and generation passes on and love/cooking the reflection of self in time. To learn, to pass on, to live beyond its many lifetimes. We just keep our wanting memories close to our heart.

A L B E R T   G A L L E G O S

Snoqualmie Falls

When I think of Snoqualmie Falls, two words come to mind, "majestic beauty." It is one of the prettiest places you will ever see.

It is located a few hours north of Seattle. You can spend the whole day pondering on its lush scenery. There is a trail that leads down to the falls, and on your way down you can take in all of the wildlife that makes its home there. Like the cute furry little squirrels that come up to you already expecting a treat and the butterflies that seem to dance in the mist coming off of the falls or the deer that hide in the trees gazing at you. It's almost as if a Walt Disney dreamscape had come to life right before your very eyes.

The moss of the rocks looks like velvet so soft that you could mistake them for little pillows on the ground. The leaves have caterpillars and other creepy crawlers traveling over them.

I would love to climb to the top of the waterfall just to see the view from up top. The mist is enchanting. The way the light passes through it is like tiny rainbows all around you. When the breeze hits the mist and carries it toward you once you feel it you are instantly refreshed.

If you feel like being transported to a different world, you should visit Snoqualmie Falls. You won't be disappointed.

I Can Fly, I Can Fly, I Can Fly

Oh, my heart, as it pounds, so heavy after every breath. No one can understand the confidence in my mind, my intentions, why I speak so as I do...when I fly. There's nothing that can stop me, no one that can beat me, not even my asthma, though I hear my soul, though I hear my soul.

As I run in the wind, through the green grass of open country, it's like releasing a giant weight off my chest and listening to the great sea. Boasting about how I was gliding, down the cliffs of the mountain's face, as I take it all in, I forget who I am—and hear, listen, understand your pace.

As I travel in time, and laugh and unwind, I gasp for air to catch my breath, awe. I pay attention to the kyanite crystal blue skies and the magnificent view from up above. The world and its wholehearted way of producing life is breathtaking enough once you listen and understand: that is when your eyes are fully open, how they reflect images of your heart scenery—picturesque—just like heaven.

Though I am exhausted, catching my air, and listening to my soul, as I fantasize—hear me loud and clear, I CAN FLY, I CAN FLY, I CAN FLY!

SAMUEL MULLIKIN

Free

I always knew I would fall. Returning to earth in an elaborate dance, a fitting final flight, lifting alone and untethered. I did not regret this knowing, nor dread its coming—those are human things. Myths about beginnings and endings.

I was hidden at a distance, my muted neutral tones a breeze swallowed by a swath of wind. We almost never met. But you stopped, happened to look down, and saw a soft curl not belonging to the earth. There I was, a piece of the sky itself, supine, resting among the rocks, staring into the blue.

Bound as you were, how could you not marvel?

In your hand I was defined by your perception, classification, and association (the hallmarks of your kind): light and soft, grey and brown and white, bird—maybe tail or wing. None of these things are really me, though, any more than the name you call me by. The world does not oblige itself to labels and boxes.

Still, some measure of what I am was apparent even if it cannot be captured with words. You perceived the edges of a dimension beyond your plane and all at once I became a novelty, a thing of beauty, a symbol you couldn't ignore. With verve, you saw aspiration in the whispers of my nature.

Thus I was taken, transported within, to a place of walls and ceilings, and doors that lock. Hidden away from the sibilant shushing of the wind, I yearned for the sun's warm glow. I do not have the indifference of stone. Such stark absences cry out in their silent way, an echo of longing trapped in negative space.

You placed me where I could be seen—a reminder of a lack of constraint, of a freedom to just *be*. You said the irony was not lost on you. I did not understand.

I am observed in quiet moments nearly every day. Sometimes I am twirled between your fingers, bringing me back for a moment to my fall from heaven. I can tell the soft brush of my velvety edge is a balm for the absences in you. Some things are universal. I do not understand this shared experience, but I sense a profoundness growing as wide as my memory of the unbroken horizon—a sense of scope barely glimpsed—a mutual resonance.

There's a growing excitement in you. A resolve that has set. I was found, you say, in a desolate patch of dirt and rocks, a place surrounded by walls of steel and stone. You understand now, you say, that I do not belong—not where I was found and not upon your wall.

I dream only of seeing the sky, once again being a witness to the great expense. I hear your fevered promises of a brighter place of wind and sun and rain. I rest in one hand while your other writes this letter—an introduction of sorts, a plea to carry through the promise you made to me. I don't understand any of it, but through that resonance, though that connection. I am given the courage and hope to believe.

I might one day *be*.

KERVON RODGERS

Back in My 'Hood

Growing up in a place most people would love to abandon; some would even say I can't wait to desert this place. When you're looking from the outside in, it would be easy for some to say the same thing. Of course, why else would people want to live in a place overrun with roaches and most people chose to sleep on the floor below the window because it's not unusual for a stray bullet to find its way in your home? Trust me, I know all too well...had a bullet hole in my sisters room right smack in the middle of the wall. Even got in trouble a few times because I used to shove gum and candy in the hole.

But let me take you on a journey and tell you why I was not ashamed to tell people where I'm from. This place taught me how to be a young man. Taught me that family is all we got. How to respect my elders which to me is a lost cause now. I grew up in an era when you said "Yes, ma'am," and "No, ma'am." I really miss those days. I can't comprehend this newer generation. In my era, a child stayed in a child's place, we watched our conduct around our elders.

I laugh when people talk about rich and poor. I know we wasn't rich, but my mama fed us three meals everyday and we always had clean clothes on our backs. They might not have been brand new, but to us there was nothing wrong with hand-me-downs. It's funny 'cause now I wouldn't dare wear someone else's clothes or shoes. But then I didn't care. If I could take a voyage back to time it would be when life was so much simpler and I understood the things around me. Back in my 'hood.

CHRISTOPHER TAYLOR

Tales of the Bayou

To take a trip, to travel, to rove the globe in which we call home is more of an innate desire than it is a luxury. If you think about it, it's in our DNA to want to explore the world. How else would one explain the spread of humanity across the earth?

One of my best experiences was a trip through the infamous Bayou. We were there for my mom, she's an Evangelist and had booked some singing engagements throughout the area. This church, that church, this side of the state, that side of the state. This is the busy hustle bustle of the movement. The idea of traveling is as unique a perspective as the person on the journey. Through their eyes, the picture is painted, each stroke an indication of past experience.

For me, the Bayou was a frightening world. Riding in the back seat as we navigated this culturally foreign land, rich in history and folklore, I couldn't help but wonder, what lies beneath. We are on a highway and the sunset is brilliant. I can feel the warmth on my skin, a slight breeze creeps through the window as we sit in heavy traffic. I hear the grown-ups conversing in the front seats about taking the service roads and something about how dangerous those back roads are. Grown up talk?

As we make our way toward the next exit, I get an uneasy feeling. At that moment, I didn't understand it, however hindsight is 20/20. The brakes squeak and the car bounces as we exit the uneven off-ramp. I look out the window eager to catch fleeting glimpses of the fading sunset, but it disappears quickly as we move onto a service road. It's dense with vegetation on both sides of the street, and I'm captivated by my own fear and imagination.

"Is this the witching hour? Is this where they do Voodoo?" Those are the things that run through my mind like Tazmanian devils. I search frantically for a sign of truth! Is what I think and dream of reality? Shadows . . . trees . . . eyes . . . cars . . . bushes . . . wait. Eyes! Whose eyes? Did I *really* see *eyes*!? My eyes, *must* be playing tricks on me. I open my mouth to ask the question "What's in these woods?" but before I could speak | EYES | peering back at me from the darkness.

"Mama!" I scream, "What boy?!" she responds, "I seen something in the woods!" Just as she turns back to me . . ." Ka-klunk!" We run over something huge and hard! "Oh my God," my mother says, as we pull off the road. "No! Don't Stop!" I say as we come to a halt. "It's okay," Mama assures me, but that falls deaf on panic-stricken ears. I close my eyes tight and begin to picture the monster that stares at little kids in the woods. He's big, mean, and hungry! My stomach is in knots, my breathing is heavy and short, and in that faintest distance, I can hear my mother trying to calm me. Footsteps outside of the car. Closer . . . even closer! And then it happens...

Juicy

Upon hearing the beat, I instantly entered the time machine . . . by the second, all of my adult features began to dissolve. I went from a scruffy beard to a tatty smooth face. Yes, once again, thirteen singing in a high pitched voice without a care in the world . . .

Sitting passenger in my cousin's raggedy Volvo, I can still feel the torn leather seats grabbing and latching on to my pants. The more you moved, the more likely you would have to unsnag yourself from the dying fabric. Hearing the young boy group Pretty Ricky's song "Juicy" made me come alive . . . Soon as it came on my body began pulsating. A huge smile would overtake my face; I would go from slouching to sitting up erect. I lack the formal skills, but I'm sure my feet were attempting to mimic a professional tap dancer. The manner in which I was able to finesse my neck with such smoothness was like a snake. It was like I didn't have any bones. I knew I thought I was on stage performing with the group from all the abrupt tears, pulls and pinches. Those damn seats were always working against me to no avail . . .

Then, my favorite part would come on which required me to channel my inner Michael Jackson and Stevie Wonder. I would belt those lines fiercely. Sadly, all it ever took was a speed dip to cause the music to come to a sudden pause. The inopportune silence would always bring me back to reality. I could never stop singing fast enough to conceal the fact that I sounded like a monkey actively being electrocuted. Man, that was the embarrassing part. All present would get a quick laugh at my expense . . .

In spite of their snickers, it only took that song being replayed for this entire process to start over again . . .

Denver Women's
Correctional Facility

N.

On August 12th, 2012, my lover and boyfriend, N., took his life with a .38 caliber revolver. Days later, when I could not reach him and was unaware of what happened, I called his mother, R. She answered and I tore into my spiel. "Hi, R., I can't get a hold of N. and I thought perhaps he was at your house visiting his boys. Could I talk to him?" A pause that cuts into me deeply from our tumultuous relationship passes as she finally responds. "You've killed him." I knew she'd come at me with something, but really? I, assuming it's metaphorical, continue with my plight undaunted. "Yes, I know you think we are killing each other in this relationship, but . . ." She interrupts. "NO. You've actually killed him. HE'S DEAD. He took his life. It's all your fault. The funeral is private, so don't plan on attending." And she hangs up before I can even process what she's said. The air literally seemed to be sucked out of the room that was now spinning. I let out a short burst of air, comparable to an almost animalistic guttural yelp, my legs wobbly. I ran to the restroom of the Village Inn I was standing in. Splashing water on my face, unaware of what exactly to do. The heavy realization that it was my fault was ringing in my ears. I'd left because I thought it was for the best. N. would continue making threats (idle, I assumed) that if I left and didn't come back, he'd kill himself, and then I'd remember him. Then I'd be with him everyday because it would be my fault for leaving. During that time, I'd listen to The Fray's "Heartless." I'd blare it alone in a haze of cigarette smoke and self-pity. I'd hear his words echo in my soul and see the deep cuts he inflicted on his thighs: "NEVER

LOVE HER" down one, "IT'S TOO MUCH" down the other. I'd flash to better times when I'd lay on his bare chest while he stroked my hair and feel the vibration of his words as he sang to me. I still can't quite recall the country song it was. Trying to recall, I had tears rolling down my face. Burning. Stinging and hot. I'd picture when we met, so full of passion, infatuation, fear, vulnerability, and hope. The sweet taste of his lips; the deep longing I felt when I'd smell his neck. I'd remember the happiness of him cooking me amazing meals. The mud-caked work boots, his t-shirts with the sleeves cut off, and his jeans. His golden baked skin calloused hard from working outside all day as a contractor. Then the whiskey bottles appeared out of nowhere. Dead soldiers coming back from an old haunt, a time we both thought had died. I'd tried for months. Condone, communicate, condemn, compromise. I'd said we'd go to our mutual corners, gain perspective, separated for a time—temporary, I'd thought. Hopeful, I'd been.

Melodic Breeze

The curtains billow in the air as the gorilla retreats out of the window, leaving behind only her eyeballs on her pillow for her parents to find. With a jolt and a gasp, she startles awake to the pounding of her heart that feels like the crescendo of the music in *Jaws* right before the shark attacks. She wishes she hadn't watched *Congo* that night.

Drowning out the panic of her heart, she forcibly sits up in her twin-sized bed and investigates the window at the head of her bed. Making sure that the window is sealed and latched, she lies back down and closes her eyes, reminding herself that it was only a dream. She opens her eyes.

With her eyes scanning the room at the beat of her heart, she begins to ground herself by finding the things she loves the most about this room. The beat slows as she recognizes the antique dressing table that's been in the family for decades. Its elegant mirrors are braced atop the painted and stressed wooden drawers and legs. The most beautiful part, to her, is the pink and white polka dot cloth that hangs like a skirt around it. As if out of body, she stares at it, treasuring it and wishing that she would look as elegant as this piece of furniture someday.

Trailing the skirt and its many dots down to the floor, she gets stuck on the brown carpet. Earlier that day, her mother had vacuumed, so this brown carpet is looking more like different shades of triangular, brown puzzle pieces. She follows each line, forming patterns and shapes in her mind's eye. One of the lines runs under the wooden dresser on the other side of the room.

On top of this dresser beseeches a porcelain music and plant box. It's been with her since her nursery days. It is too late to rotate the dial of the music box, so she regards the pastel pink and blue paint on this box while trying her best to remember the heavenly melody it would play. She practices and practices humming the sweet melody until she feels like she gets it right.

Finally, her gaze rests on her favorite part of this room. She doesn't know why she adores the wallpaper as much as she does. Not far from where her head heats up the pillow is a strip of this wallpaper that runs in a continuous line all around the room. First, the alphabet A-Z, then numbers 0-9. Over and over they repeat themselves. She musically whispers the alphabet from the previous melody to herself over and over again until the letters gracefully begin to float around on the wall. Her eyes trail in circles and swirls as these letters create beautiful designs. She tries to see how many words she can come up with. Cat. Dog. Cow. The. Box...Before she knows it, she's forgotten all about the gorilla and her eyeballs left on her pillow. Mom. Dad. Love. Brothers...She burrows deeper under her covers and drifts off into another land of peace and happiness. Her eyes close and she is finally able to re-welcome the darkness as the peaceful hum in her heart lulls her back to sleep.

Homesick

Nostalgia. Or, otherwise said, homesick. Over the years, you have danced through my thoughts.

Do you remember all the memories we made together? All that time ago, two kids, reckless and limitless. At times, messy and unkind. Nevertheless, always loyal to one another.

Somewhere along the way, I heard it's not enough to just learn something, you must live it also. Learn it. Live it.

For us, it was a sordid voyage of living and learning.

There are so many memories I cherish. To name a few . . .

Going down to the river on hot summer days . . . Halloween parties . . . coloring your hair bright pink and mine all different colors . . . . driving in my grandma's red truck with the music up all the way and the windows down . . .

"Your tears don't fall
They crash around me."

I still proudly wear the tattoo you and I got together. I always wonder if you do too.

For the longest time, my only focus was on all the bad and painful shit we went through. As if we only had bad times. In hindsight, we had way more to live for than I ever saw.

Even though I was toxic for you most of the time, you never gave up on me. Loving another and being loved were out of reach.

Still, you held my hand.

You chose me.

All the while, I chose everyone else. Viewing it today from a healthier frame of mind, it hurts me knowing I did that to you. Not to say you did no wrong in our friendship, but you were definitely the better half.

All these years of our time apart has only caused a more prominent desire to be with you again.

Our souls are joined; forever in a world where nothing lasts.

Soulmates. Best friends.

As my soul aches for you it aches also for home.

Nostalgic and homesick.

You are my home.

D E N I S E   E L L I O T T

The Feather

As I float to the ground below at a leisurely speed, I feel fear. I am a single feather, detached from my eagle, my glorious mother. The wind catches me. I'm swirling, tumbling, descending. I gently land on the warm red dirt. New Mexico is so hot in the summer. What am I now? A single feather laying here. I can see my graceful host flying over me as I lay here. I am a great symbol of this glorious bird, the eagle. I hear someone coming, a native man. He picks me up. I feel his warm hands rustle through my strands. As he examines me, I feel his respect. He carries me and sets me on a rustic wooden table. What is my future? He starts to add things to me: turquoise and bright beads with a strand of leather. I can feel the heat from the glue. He is decorating me with his tribe's colors. When he is done, I'm a stunning creation. He hangs me from a mirror in his truck. I feel the warm sun through the window. This is my new birth. I hang here as a symbol of respect from the native people. This is my new home. I'm no longer afraid.

Cowboy China

It was a steel, somber 14th of February, 1950. While everyone in the country was still trying to gather their bearings, just coming out of one war and headed into another, my Papa was gathering his bride. Home on leave from the navy, he seized his opportunity to marry the best gal this side of the Continental Divide. It was a modest affair, but a monumental day that neither of them took lightly for the next 55 years. One of the few wedding presents they received was a Westward Ho collection. Plates, bowls, cups, and even salt-and-pepper shakers were parts of this western cowboy set. Those dishes represented a lifestyle. Outlined with brands, painted with a variation of backing horses, saddles, and other western themes, those dishes reflected the elements that make Kenney hearts tick. Waste not, want not, every meal was served on those dishes. Living through the Great Depression, WWI and WWII, my Manga and Papa took pride that they had three meals to serve on that Cowboy China. When I was six, my Papa and Dad bought property together, so I also got to eat every meal on those plates. It was those times that I learned about life: how to have manners, how to have a conversation, and how important core connections are. When Manga and Papa passed away, their estate was divided between their children and grandchildren. They left their Cowboy China to me. Those 70-year-old dishes continue to instill tradition, learning, lifestyle, comfort, support during hardship, and everlasting love.

LISA LESYSHEN

End of Everything

Little did I know that "before and after" would soon define my life. How is it that someone needs to be taught to sit in a chair? You are an adult, it should be easy, it should be automatic, it should be simple. But when you attempt to sit in the chair, it is anything but simple. It feels like you are sitting on a triangle of jello requiring you to balance precariously. You see-saw back-and-forth; you see-saw side-to-side. Never stable, always wobbly, so unsettled, so unhinged. You have to take a break from trying to sit up. How pathetic is that? The constant drum of despair thumps in the back of your skull questioning if you are strong enough to do this. Your mind whirls with questions that carry no easy answers. You wish you had at least one answer, one directive, one guideline that might help you find your way. Find your way back to your life you knew before.

Everyone loves a story of transformation about the underdog who triumphs over adversity. I was unsure if this would be part of my story, if I had the grit to make that a part of my life.

The last thing I remembered was the rain drizzling on my face as they wheeled my body over our deck. They had ripped my wedding rings off my finger that had been on my finger for 25 years and they would never grace my finger again. There were no bright lights nor were there singing angels. There was only darkness. A deep black abyss. I would soon learn the true meaning of hell on earth. When I woke up, the world had turned gray and I would soon experience a profound sorrow that would be unrelenting. The grim reality that my life had been forever changed had not settled in my mind yet.

They tell you to straighten your back and push back your shoulders, that these skills will enable you to sit in the chair successfully. You try to comply with their directives, but you feel the heat start to erupt in your feet. It sweeps upward to your stomach and finally explodes in your head causing you to be transported to the beach. It is a soothing escape, the turquoise water, the warmth of the sun combines with the smooth, white sand. This is where you go when it becomes too much, unbearable. Never did you think it would be so excruciating attempting to sit upright in a chair. Unfortunately, you will never be able to escape the consequences of that night and you will never cease trying to get back to where you were before. You never knew it would be this difficult, and you will never be able to make sense of it. The only thing that was certain was that they were going to make you try and try again to sit upright in that damn wheelchair.

Hungry Eyes

My grandfather "Bum Bum," with his weathered, wrinkled nape like crocodile skin, had his twisted hand gripping the neck of a well-worn guitar, calloused fingers gently strumming over the strings. Other old men with time-etched faces, cradling their own instruments: guitar, banjo, mandolin, spoons for tapping out a beat.

I am sitting with Grammie on the old, soft, blue couch. Whispering in my ear, she admonishes me to keep quiet and still as a mouse while these men practice the music that keeps their histories, roots, cultures, and ancestors alive. Twangy, toe-tapping bluegrass, old country and gospel standards. Uncle Earl announces they will perform a song entitled "Hungry Eyes." I remember that name because it sounds so funny to my youthful, innocent ears. As ol' Bill sings the words:

"Mama never had the luxuries she wanted

But it wasn't 'cause my daddy didn't try.

She only wanted things she really needed;

One more reason for my mama's hungry eyes."

I notice Bum Bum's eyes—red-rimmed and shiny. The tears roll down his raw sunburned cheeks to splash like dark blossoms on his plain snap shirt. Grammie roughly pulls me close to her with her arm around my shoulders, tugging my braids—a closeness not common. When the last chord fades, Bum Bum turns away and mops his face with his big red hanky.

The peculiar displays of emotion frighten me. My belief in the security and immutability of my grandparents shaken. I run home and dad pulls me onto his lap and says that sometimes the old songs bring up memories of hard times the folks went through. He says we will talk about it some other time—but we never do.

***

A few years later . . . Studying Nebraska history, learning about the ravages of the Dust Bowl and Great Depression, reading my beloved *Grapes of Wrath* for the first time. An old black and white photograph, captioned "Migrant Mother." A dark-haired woman dressed in worn-out, frayed clothing with her thin fingers clutching at her gaunt face, creases tracing through her leathered skin, a far-off gaze of sorrow and defeat. The very epitome of hungry eyes. Two raggedy children, faces hidden from the camera, clinging to her for comfort. And reminding me so poignantly of the few sepia photos I've seen of my dad's childhood. Snippets of hushed, solemn conversations at family gatherings, not meant for younger ears. How my great grandmother was buried with her 21st baby in her arms ". . . milk fever and not havin' a pot to piss in and just bein' used up." Grammie getting pregnant at 16 to get out of her house where there were too many mouths to feed. Grammie and Bum Bum loading up all their meager possessions into their Model A with Dad and Lois in the back, the twins held on Grammie's lap for the five-day trip to Idaho to pick fruit. How they all returned to Alliance after the war started because Bum Bum could get WPA work building the Army air base.

*

More years later . . . I see Merle Haggard on TV performing "Hungry Eyes" at the Grand Ole Opry. He humbly stands with his guitar like a babe in arms and softly croons the haunting lyrics. And I am thrown back to my grandparents' basement and the performance that affected them so deeply. A hard bubble of regret fills me, chokes me, and brings the tears to my eyes. I miss my grandparents so much, both gone for so long, and wish I had known them better and honored them more. I finally begin to grasp the hard work, the courage and grit, the sacrifices of body, mind, heart, and will—the strength—that eventually delivered me to this comfortable, self-indulgent life.

LACIE NELSON

Uprooted

I was once surrounded by beautiful flowers, garden tools and people who watered me. Then the day came when I was picked up and taken from my once-beautiful fresh environment and placed in a small dark space that had no sunlight, no people talking to you, or at you. There was no one looking at me saying how green my leaves are or how big I was getting. All of it was gone.

Minutes became hours, hours became days, days became weeks. There was no one and I was so very thirsty. My once luscious forest-green leaves began to shrivel and harden. It was not long before my leaves turned a terrible poop-brown color. I used to be over a foot tall and now I was only a couple inches. I was starving and could hardly breathe. My nutrients were done, I had nothing left. I am dust.

CHRIS NYE

Night Sky Falling

I look out my window and the moon aglow, just hanging effortlessly in the deep black liquid sky. All the stars freckled across it, as if blown from a tender gentle kiss from the palm that held onto them all day, keeping them safe.

Oh, how I long to be outside at night. Swallowed by the vast openness. Listening to the sounds night makes. The wind gently kissing my face. But there is this sound—without sound. So peaceful, the air so crisp, so cool, whispering to the trees all its secrets. At night, the air just seems so fresh. Every midnight a fresh new day starts.

All my days roll into one in here. They all look the same 50 shades of white and the new meaning of 50 shades of gray. Whether it be new paint, old paint, clean paint, dirty paint, fresh paint, or chipped paint. It all determines the shade. Sparingly, there are also the hints of penitentiary green. But if you look closely, one other color emerges here and there, everywhere.

Rust! This beautiful reddish, orangish, brownish color brings a little outside in. When you think of rust, you think of metal being treated with water over a period of time.

How can this be? These splashes of rust everywhere. No water—

I ponder this thought and come up with my own conclusion. I remember lying awake many a night, listening to the sobs in the night, all the salty tears falling. I look around in the day, and I can see the salty tears falling. This place soaking it all up. Many nights I've cried into a damp pillowcase. Many times, tears rolling down my face, running to hide themselves in the droplets of water that shower my body every day. Cleaning not just my body, but cleaning my soul! I look down and see more rust surrounding the hole my tears escape to.

Instead, I would give anything to be in the night sky crying tears of joy, being washed clean by the rain—

At times, I feel the night sky falling on me.

Chlorine

In a small suburb of Denver, I found summers were best spent with my best friends at our local rec center. I remember the smell of chlorine and how later in life that very smell would always transport me back to that rec center. My friends and I would always throw colored rings in the pool and then we would see who could find them the fastest. That rec center, with sounds of squeaking basketball courts and "thwack" sounds of the racket ball courts, was always a safe haven for us kids. The smell of chlorine, now, transports me back to a place of innocence. A place where being a latchkey kid was acceptable and spending hours outside without checking in was a catalyst for a truly memorable childhood. Twenty-two years later I find myself back at that same rec center aiding my toddler in her little tumbler class. Walking back in that building with the chlorine hitting my senses. Once again I find myself playing "find it" at the bottom of the pool and not having a care in the world.

DENISE PRESSON

If, By Chance

The wave of anxiety wrenches my guts, twisting like the sobs of grief gripped and tugged five years ago in that sterile cold jail cell. Each step towards the dog's owner now reminded me of how my deep inhales wrung my soul. Twisting, squeezing the vice of my choices. Each step, each wave a contraction that would deliver me from this reality. Every footfall—advancing, pushing me towards the stranger who could not, would not know the genesis of the pain. Pores being squeezed of insecurity, shame, judgment, ego, pain...so much suffering. Miserably social graces are exchanged with this sweet kind-faced stranger. This visitor that entrusted...me, a prisoner, a murderer, with her pet, her companion, her beloved dog.

Never do we consciously map the long-reaching destination of a momentary choice.

Would I know the agony I convulsed with years before today be for the death of my mother or for my own child that would attempt to end her own life. Would this outsider know her choice be a soothing salve to my soul.

Every word that exits my mouth is a tipped ewer pouring the moisture of anxiety from my brow and lip. The cold of prison and this visiting room is no match for the heat of my nerves. Apologetic for the stream of emotions I dab at my face only to humiliatingly leave bits of tissue stuck to my face.

Sorrow led me here to this room, to this woman, all seemingly by chance but not so. Each briny drop of sadness does not bring him back, does not restore all that was destroyed.

I stumble through my presentation of a behavior her beloved Duke has shown me and I named it "Ostrich." As I speak, her kind face brightens in knowing her dog has squeezed his head in my lap so I can smooth his pot-holders-for-ears on my seated thighs for comfort. Comfort that Duke gives to her upon her returns every night from work.

As we allow the bridge this dog has built to settle between us, she offers me more toilet paper and words. Words of reassurance and support for the prison canine program. I see, in the light of this moment, how much darkness this soul, this beautiful soul in front of me doesn't see. If, by chance, we all can feel the salve, the healing, from one choice.

CASSANDRA RIEB

Invisible Waves

Chaos and confusion restrain her. Too heavy and unbearable, she closes her eyes as anxiety captures her. She presses a button and adjusts a dial. Invisible waves find her, filling her from head to toe. She responds involuntarily—bobbing her head, tapping her foot. Harmonies and dissonant chords flow rhythmically around and blossom within, beginning her escape. It reaches and grows, with breath-stealing rests, building crescendos and quickening tempos. Now that it's found her, she is set free.

Felt more vividly than any physical sensation, music carries her. It holds her. Capable of depriving, capable of replenishing, music gives life to emotion. It unburies her pain and releases her anguish. Music is her therapy. It speaks to her more coherently than words.

In her world, music has a life of its own. Childhood fairy tales pale in comparison to the stories notes tell. Songs, indelibly written on her soul, remain there forever. Melodies wrap around her, tucking her in at night. Music is the one and only constant that has always been and will always be there. She and the song are one.

The variations of music's expression find her. Each moment has its own beautiful tune. It saves her every day, life's symphonious concerto.

Bars

Looking up at the ceiling, the bars of the fences outside cast a harrowing shadow. It's fitting bars should continue to play a role in my life. I've gone from liquor bars, to barred windows, to prison bars. Each attempt to destroy the role of one concept of the word in my life succeeds only to be replaced by a less desirable sort.

A. My earliest childhood memory is of my sister and I playing tag in a bar. We were three and four years old! The party just raged on around us as we weaved around the legs of strangers. Pink, orange, and yellow lights surging and flashing through the darkness as disco hits boomed through the speakers. My mom was a party girl of the 80s. No babysitter, no problem! She just brought us along to work.

When she married my stepdad, who was in the Navy, not much changed. We didn't go along anymore, but they brought the party home. The house became the bar, flashing lights, darkness, strangers, liquor. It also became a battlefield. Us kids marking our territory and defending its boundaries from potential enemies. Some battles were lost. And innocence lost along the way. By age 12, I became the bartender at these at-home bars. My parents moved around a lot, so their friends changed, but the party was always the same. I ran away at age 14.

I guess this is the ugly road that led to my current demise.

Looking at the ceiling, I watch the shadows fade into darkness. Ready and waiting to once again leave the bars behind me. Hopefully the choices I make in the future keep me free.

B. My first apartment had bars on the windows. I was living in Center City, Philadelphia. A most desirable location for gays in the 90's. I was 17. I finally got a job I could tell my grandma the truth about. I even had decent hours: 6 a.m. to 2 p.m., Monday through Friday.

No more dancing. No more late nights. No more couchsurfing. From now on, I was going to be living the good life...or so I thought. No one tells you life gets harder as you get older. At least, no one told me. It seemed I would take one step forward and two steps back.

I got my GED, but then I got arrested for marijuana and had to pay a huge fine. I started college, I "fell in love," moved away to accommodate him, and had a baby. I got back into school, I got married to an abusive alcoholic, found myself back in a bar bartending, becoming what I hated as a kid: a numbed out, oblivious, negligent, always drunk-and-high parent.

When I get sober and divorced, I find myself in yet another apartment with bars on the windows, this time in a less than desirable neighborhood in Daytona Beach. I also have three more kids and a life without direction, purpose, or ambition. Sobriety didn't last long, but the drugs had "changed." Prescription meds still allowed me to function highly as a parent involved at my kids' schools, work two jobs, but I was still making terrible relationship choices.

Even the decision to break free from the meds didn't keep me from seeking love in all the wrong places.

But now I know it was how I tried to get free. I couldn't do it alone. I tried so many times. Behind these bars, I wasn't alone. Breaking the cycle isn't easy, the cycle is easy. It runs on momentum. Now that I'm not alone, I've done it. And I know, when I move from behind these fences, I will finally be free from bars.

C. The first time I was arrested, I stole some Binaca. I was 14. My best friend and I were out shopping at the NEX with my mom. We used to lift all kinds of stuff from this place, but never were we with a parent.

Breath spray. Anyway, they caught us, walked us through the store where my mom saw us, and down a hallway to a small office.

What could have just been a light talking to, turned into so much more. Mom caught up with the guard. She somehow convinced him to get the MP's involved. So next thing you know, we were sitting side by side in the back of the cop car on our way to the brig.

They put us into a day cell with a drain in the center of the room. We hadn't said one word to another until Adrienne finally broke the silence, "I wonder what Beavis and Butthead would do in our situation." We both lost it.

When we finally recovered from our fit, her parents, my parents and an officer were at the door. In front of us, they gave our parents the choice of sending us to 30 days reform school or being released to them. I gave Adrienne a reassuring look knowing it was my mom who orchestrated this whole thing anyway. Who would watch the kids when they went out this weekend? I knew we were about to get out.

Her parents grounded her for a month. They were straight-edged so she did the whole month. I was off restriction by the weekend. I wasn't allowed to babysit while I was grounded and they needed to party.

Thus, began my life of crime. My arrest record isn't lengthy, but over time became progressively worse: car theft, expunged; drug possession, expunged; drug paraphernalia, expunged. And so on.

I turn 40 this week, praise the goddess, maturity and sobriety rule the next 40 years of my life. I'm ready to bar the bars from my future.

NICHOLE ROSHTO

Buzz

As a young child in base housing on Andrews Air Force Base, before my parents' divorce, there were many bees. My parents had an old, decaying shed in the backyard that served as a nest for wood bees. I developed an intense fear of insects, despite never being stung by one. I attribute never being stung largely to the fact that I never went outside. I was an eight year old with agoraphobia. The closest I got to playing outside for several years was watching TV in our sunroom. If I did perchance venture outside, because my parents didn't want to leave me alone while they ran errands, I ran at the slightest sound of a buzzing noise. Usually it was subsequently discovered to be buzzing in my ear.

These days, my fear of bees has slowly ceased. I've been stung by wasps. I don't let my fear keep my inside or running from buzzing noises anymore. Every now and then the sight of a bee in the summer still makes my skin crawl.

Pride

Up until this point in her life, she was actually pretty smart, ambitious, and strong-minded. She was untouchable, unafraid. At 20 years old, she had just given birth to identical twin boys and was in college working on EMT certifications. She was so determined to make a life for herself that she walked her happy butt right into a military recruiter's office, ready to sign her life away. The Air Force was her first choice. That didn't happen because they don't accept single parents, so she settled for the Navy. From that day forward, the training started. If her memory is correct, there were just five of them in that delayed enlistment program. They would be up at 5 a.m. every day, running laps, and doing push-ups at the Air Force Academy. She never made it to the Navy. All of that training, months of studying, and every ounce of pride she felt for herself all flew out the window the second those handcuffs clicked on her on that mountain road.

It's weird how this world works though. From that moment on, her life slowly declined into a pit of pain and despair. All of that strength, hope, ambition dwindled into nothing. And just when she was at her darkest in prison, that hope started to return. This place forces you to have a strength of mind, and it also forces you to make a better life. When she first got here, it was almost natural to her to start working out and training like she was back then, before life hit her. She is slowly finding herself again, even if she has to start from nothing. But she knows she wants to work toward that feeling of pride and accomplishment that she once felt.

Lynn Young

Magic and Marshmallow

As a little girl who still believed in fairy tales and happily-ever-afters, I could never imagine the impact Grandma's house would have on me for the rest of my life.

My grandma's house was a charming quaint house that had the same alluring pull of the Hansel and Gretel cottage of candy. It was sweet innocent magic. It has a grand front porch with an old gentle swing on it. When you sat down, it would take you anywhere you could dream of. All the bushes around the porch grew the whitest, sweetest smelling snowballs. I love the sweet smell of the yard in spring and summer. Inside the house was warm and safe because of the fairy grandmother living inside.

My great grandma was a plump old woman who was so gentle and soft. She taught me to believe in the good of people. I loved when my mom dropped me off there. It's the house that I learned some of the greatest life lessons. At a small simple kitchen table with an old marble chess set.

There wasn't anything spectacular about the chess set, but it was everything to me. The pieces were chipped and warm with age and being used all the time. In fact, they looked cold, but they always shocked me with how warm they felt.

I always wanted to be at my great grandma's house. She gave the best hugs. Her house smelled of snowballs. She was my best friend. I miss her so much.

At seven, I loved to sit at that kitchen table and play chess all day.

Oh no, it wasn't the actual game that excited me, even though I enjoyed it. It wasn't even the chocolate marshmallow cookies at the end of each game.

It was those soft gentle brown eyes that poured out all the love one little girl could dream of. It was the smile that lit up the world brighter than any supernova could. Her laugh was sweeter than any bird song.

She taught me how to be kind and love everyone. Everyone you meet is fighting a battle you know nothing about; show compassion. The lesson that has stuck with me through everything is, no matter how hard things will ever get, she taught me to work through it. Even out of the darkest moments good things will come from it, even if you can't see it at the time. How could she teach me all this at such a young age. A chessboard and cookies. After all, she was a fairy godmother.

No, she didn't always let me win, because that's not how real life really happens. But win or lose, I always got the cookie, because the sweetest reward in life is trying. I am thankful she taught me it's okay to lose, but don't give up.

By 37, I still live by those lessons. I realize how blessed I was to have the relationship I had with her. My great grandma was an amazing woman who I miss so much. Thirty years doesn't heal the loss of losing her.

Four Mile
Correctional Facility

Transported

I remember being ten years old, riding in the back of my mom's car the first time that I remember hearing the song "Bohemian Rhapsody" by Queen. My mom drove an older grey Firebird, the one with the T-top, a very fast car for a young mother of two. So she had picked up my brother and I from our babysitter fairly late—my mom was working as a waitress at America's Bar and Grill at the time—and we were driving home when the song came on. The intro immediately caught my attention—it was weird and whimsical, and it had my young mind's full attention. I remember feeling like I was strapped into a rocket ship watching the stars fly by overhead (I loved the T-top as a kid). The feeling of being pushed into the seats as my mom accelerated away from a stoplight. The rough seatbelt and not very comfortable material of the seats against the bare skin of my arms. The combination of rock and roll and classical music plus Freddie Mercury's own twist on both created a song that still transports me back to that happy place in my childhood.

BRIAN JAMES LEE

Splash

Watching as the sun comes up, its warmth washing over me, I still feel the chill left from the fleeing night. Everything the same, always the same. For centuries I have sat here in the same spot, immune to the tests of time, one stone among many overlooking the same lake. Animals come and go; plants sprout and grow under the sun. For me, my existence has become numb. As I lull in and out of lucidity, I notice something new, it appears to be an animal walking upright on two legs, mostly hairless except a patch right on top of his head, swinging two appendages from the side of its body as it walks. Enamored by something new, I can't take my attention off of him (it). I watch as he gets closer: he is looking down kicking rocks around. He is almost on top of me and he pulls his leg back to kick me, but pauses mid-kick and reaches down. His hand moves closer and closer, blotting out the sun as his fingers close and wrap around me. I can't hardly believe it. I feel the warmth of his hand and the steady rhythm of his beating heart as I am lifted higher and higher. I see his face up close as we take measure of each other. He nods to me (I'm not sure why), then puts me in his right hand, his index finger wrapping around me as he cocks his hand back . . . And flings his arm forward releasing me. The world becomes a blur. I am flying through the air at an incredible speed as fast as a falcon diving for its prey. I cut through space and time on a journey unlike any other. I have not experienced where I will end up, I do not know . . . I . . . SMACK . . . I hit the water with an amazing force and am shot back up into the air, once again king of the sky, master of speed, conqueror of . . . SMACK! I hit the water again with enough speed to be launched back into the air. Gravity unable to contain me soaring free. I see everything from a new perspective, the world slowing down . . . SPLASH . . . I am wet. Enveloped in cold water, I sink. Watching the light above me grow darker and darker until I land softly on the earth at the bottom of the lake. It's almost too much to process. I feel alone again, more than I ever have. I feel so lucky to have been chosen for that grand adventure, out of all my brother and sister stones. I alone have mastered gravity, rose above my station in this existence and flew. Transcending my old life, I am now awoken to a new plane of awareness, excited for what the universe has in store for me.

Life and Death on the Prairie

We were a quarter mile from our great uncle's cabin, snow covered the world, a cold wet mass that clung to the grooves of my shoes and turned my gloved fingers to icicles. Our great uncle's ranch housed many animals, but for some unexplainable reason, we were enthralled with the cows. They were grand lumbering beasts, black and white, just as every child knew they would be. We decided to follow them like little hunters intent on closing the distance. Could we pet them? Maybe ride them? Our Mom would be so surprised if we came back riding them. Our minds were wild with unlimited possibilities.

The closer we got to the cows, the quicker they sped away. Were they afraid of us? Four small boys aged five to ten with long dark hair cascading down our backs hunched low, stalking. A testament to our ancestors. Maybe something in their bovine genome harkened back to a primeval time, hunters and the hunted. I wanted to call out to them, "Don't be afraid. Our people hunted Buffalo, not cows." But why would they listen to me? We were stalking them.

An hour of freezing misery, and a lot of, "I'm cold. Can we go?" later, we hadn't gotten any closer. Our ancestors would be disappointed. That's when I came up with a brilliant idea. "If we cross the frozen river, we can get in front of them. Climb a tree, wait for them to pass under, and jump down on them." I looked to my brothers to see what they thought. I found no dissent.

The river wasn't wide, about twenty feet, but how deep was it? We had no idea. We had watched the cows cross the ice, so it had to be safe, right? We scrabbled down the embankment, snow heavy and wet, stole its way into my gloves, over the tops of my shoes, and down the backside of my pants, but we made it. We were on the river. The ice was a slick sheet of frosted glass that we fought, to keep our footing. I had found a large stick, and begin prodding the ice. If it was too thin or rotten, my stick would punch a hole. Like a WWII soldier with a mine detector, I swept and tapped the ice trying to find the safest way across. "Don't go past this point," I declared as I punched a hole into the ice. "It's too thin."

About halfway across my older brother decided to test the ice I had told him was too thin. He strode past me with all the bravado a ten year old could possess. "See, it's g—," the ice cracked a warning like thunder, then gave way. The black depths took my brother. Swallowed him whole. He was gone. I was only two feet away. I could have—should have—reached out and pulled him back. I didn't. I froze. I froze like the ice: cold and immobile. I stared at the hole unable to do anything. I never heard my little brothers say anything. Ice doesn't have ears. Bubbles burst from the hole. HIS LAST BREATH, HIS LAST BREATH! terror cried in my mind as tears of ice froze to my cheeks.

Water shot from the churning hole. I saw him flailing. He burst from the grip of the watery grave, fell back on the ice trying to find purchase. Again, I was supposed to help. I didn't. I was ice, a sculpture of a coward. The ice rejected his weight and gave way. He sunk, again disappearing below the ice. His cries cut off by the life stealing cold of the water.

The world held its breath as the wind cried, cried with a coward. I cried for my brother lost under the ice. I also cried for something inside myself. Something I didn't know if I would ever find again. Once more the water churned. My brother shot from the hole, a testament to his will to live. He grasped, searching the ice for anything, or anyone to help him. Finally my body gave way to will. I dropped to the ice taking my brother by the arms, I pulled him from the maw. He was so cold he could barely move. We took off his soaked coat and gave him all of our dry ones.

We walked back to our great uncle's cabin, no cows, no parade. Just four freezing boys happy we were alive.

Fremont Correctional
Facility

Point Judith

Point Judith, for Mr. Aurelio, is a small area in Narragansett, Rhode Island, that is an essential place of his childhood. Between the 1980's and 1990's, Mr. Aurelio's mother, uncle and aunt each owned a small beach house on a small piece of property in this very active, small, private community, resting soundly on the ocean coast.

Point Judith was a forty-five minute drive south of Mr. Aurelio's hometown, Providence, Rhode Island. This is where Mr. Aurelio grew up with his brother and sisters. Mr. Aurelio and his family spent a lot of time in Point Judith, especially on the weekends and summer break from school.

From the deck of the beach house, Mr. Aurelio could see the private beach, a few hundred yards away, the break walls, Block Island in the distance, ferry boats giving tours, water skiers, fishing boats, seagulls in the sky, and the endless, vast ocean. This view, the minute he arrived, filled him with pure enthusiasm, adrenaline and endless excitement.

One reason why Mr. Aurelio was filled with pure enthusiasm, and pure excitement, was due to, not only the exquisite views and delicious seafood, but all the incredible sounds, smells and fun, endless fun.

Within a few hundred feet of Point Judith, you could smell and hear the salty Atlantic Ocean, the aroma of seafood and BBA in the air, tanning oil, endless laughter, children playing in the distance, the waves crashing into the break wall and shore, the chirps from seagulls and you knew all the fun was feet away.

Once Mr. Aurelio and his family arrived at the beach house, they had to unpack the car which Mr. Aurelia and his brother typically were responsible for doing before heading to the beach. Mr. Aurelio and his brother had a routine for throwing everything on the porch and taking off.

Mr. Aurelio and his brother would drag out the cooler, beach chairs and anything they were responsible for taking to and from the beach. Of course, they would also bring buckets and goggles to hunt for crabs.

On the walk down to the beach, they would plan their day. They would discuss swimming, crab hunting, making sandcastles, fishing, eating, running up and down the beach, looking for who caught the biggest fish on the break wall and playing. This would happen over and over again, until they had to leave. The brothers never followed any pattern.

Typically, around noon time, the Point Judith Ferry would come within a couple hundred feet of our shoreline and honk their horn, it was loud. Mr. Aurelio and his brother both knew it was time for lunch.

By that time their day was half over. However, Mr. Aurelio knew their reward by the end of the day was chowder and clam cakes at Aunt Carrie's Food Restaurant then an ice cream cone.

By the end of the day Mr. Aurelio and his brother would have to carry all their belongings back to the beach house, which was tiresome, especially after spending all day in the sun. Mr. Aurelio and his brother knew it was close to the time to head back home to the city where they would both desperately wait till the next time they could come to the beach.

Mr. Aurelio truly misses the taste of salt water in his mouth, the painful sunburns, Aunt Carrie's Sea Food, all the fun he experienced and shared with his brother.

Point Judith, the beach house, the drive to-and-from, the endless fun with family and friends and all these memories, will never be lost.

BROCK BUTSON

Hummingbird

Spring, 2004. Mom's patio, Idaho. Too early for hummingbirds; the feeders full anyway. Just in case, maybe. Or hoping for a miracle? The daily hospice visit over, the news dire, however expected. Mom wheeled outside to smoke. Forty years she's been smoking, her once moist and pristine insides now as dry and ravaged as the crepe paper skin of her outside. Sixty, way too young to die, I think, watching her light up again.

I lack relationship skills. Reasons why vary but tend to revolve around abandonment issues. Mom came and went from my life like spring blossoms. I have eyes though, and they notice things, even if keeping most of what they see to myself. Like how hummingbird art outnumbers pictures of me by about 100-to-1. Seems hummingbirds replaced men like men replaced me, yet here I was sitting alone with her at the end. Life's sense of humor on full, unapologetic display. This whole dying thing is new to both of us. Even her own parents were still living. We were keeping conversation academic and impersonal, but hearing death was imminent caused us to shift. The nurse's voice still echoed around us. "Leave nothing about life unasked or unspoken," she urged, "or you'll regret it." Meaning me, I figured, considering Mom wouldn't be around to regret anything.

Turned out we both wanted to ask something substantial of the other. Not about life, though—about death. I wanted to ask Mom to try and contact me from the other side, should she discover there is one. To let me know she was safe. And she wanted me "to make damn sure" she didn't suffer. I could still hear the nurse, her prediction ominous. Mom would soon lose consciousness and her pain would spiral out of control. And then she made it clear that enough medicine was provided to ensure Mom wouldn't need to "suffer needlessly" and admonished me not to hold back on dosages.

Mom agreed to contact me from the other side in a way I couldn't miss in return of my promise to "take care of it." I knew exactly what she meant and wasn't about to be specific. Which of us was asking more of the other? Neither seemed either simple or easy. As it turned out the nurse did provide enough medicine to do the job. The minutes it took for the drugs to take full effect felt like hours, with Mom's frail hands engulfed in my own, torrents of tears streaming from our eyes.

Spring 2010. My patio, Colorado. A tiny hummingbird of iridescent green appears from out of nowhere. First to ever visit my home. No feeders and that early in April, no flowers. A female, I knew, without knowing how. She hovered at eye level, our unblinking eyes just inches from each other's. Time stood still until I said, "Thanks, Mom, I'm glad you're okay."

Then, as if to prove it was her, she flew away.

WILLIAM CONEY

Silly Putty

Time moves like Silly Putty when you're young. It stretches forever, then reclaims its primordial egg-like shape. When pressed, small handprints on one side expose images on the other. Constant pressure and stress will create distortion. My image had to decrease distortion by dampening the stress the little ones would endure.

The children needed something to hold onto, something more tangible than me. I wanted them to judge for themselves, become my critics. Only then could they understand I wasn't leaving them. S— was still in pull-ups, so D— only 18 months older, represented them. He delivered a pragmatic speech on the precipice of tears. They reached for me, but their tiny, obstructed handprints landed side by side on a visiting window slightly larger than an envelope on end. I was looking back at them, while looking at life and 30. I caught my reflection in this small window, and summoned my final microgram of strength. Composing myself, behind the persona of an archetypal father, I accepted the Pokémon commission.

My children seemed pacified with the promise, and turned away, their departure obscured by the little handprint smudges and the upwelling end of my stoic reflection. They walked off hand in hand without looking back. On their third step, I started to pull out my hair. I needed a paint brush and I needed it fast. My hair was the perfect length, but only in the front. A minor makeover supplied just enough to stuff into a pen barrel.

The jailhouse art studio consisted of a badly abused stainless-steel table, displaying six cups of syrupy separated colors and a handmade paint brush. A killer and a cat burglar consulted me on the anatomy of Pikachu, shot caller for the Pokémon. The pigments were stripped from M&M's, allowing the experts to take payment in soggy chocolate-covered tailings. This was serious business, I listened intently as they chewed.

I became an artist that day, and my first painting was easily the most important piece I ever rendered. It was my word, my image, the only thing left for them to hang onto, and everything I am now. The experts taught me a few things, but I listened to the critics. Brush strokes seemed to say more than words could, especially to preschoolers. As the years passed, I continued to paint to please the critics. They were my life, my world, my everything. Subject matter and selected shades of the requests told more than a visit would permit. As they matured so did the compositional juxtapositions. They taught me the fine details: how time is harmonized with color and applied with care. One of my critics took up the brush and used it incredibly well. I hoped she would realize that the time I spent with their projects was my only way of spending time with them.

I paid more attention to the details, to show my love. My final lesson was on the illusion of perspective, and how it's not all about me.

The critics walked away without looking back again. Perhaps they wonder if an artist can use a pen for its intended purpose, to tell them they're missed. They have each other, and now, I have art. I hope I am mature enough for this juxtapositional composition, because time moves like Silly Putty when you're not.

GREGORY FREILINGER

How One Should Be Loved

With that one person you absolutely will not live without, you have no choice but to overlook one's imperfections. By loving that one (me) you set your insight in an eclectic manner which allows you to see beyond ones yesterday. In doing so, you forgive what used to be the past and appreciate, cherish, and treasure the value of the enormous amount of love you share. By loving me, you sir—yes, you—must not withdraw your state of mind, or allow others to fog your perspective and attention on just how dear I am to you. You never permit such a weakness to stand between our love or fill our resilient light. In order to love me, you have to understand it's not just about you and your own way anymore, it's about what you can give up or take in to make everything you love about us last. You're part of a whole, you're the other half, you see something that's concerning to the other, you find a median amongst each other. You must not make the other hurt in such a way you begin to see and feel or let revenge has take play and teach its lessons. At the end of the day, you must make sure the other has comfort and sleep, knowing just how special the other is. To see the other suffer is hate, not love. Love and hate. Both four letter words. Which do you see yourself evolving into for that one special person he has come to live for?

E Z E K I E L   G A R C I A

The Mouse Trap

I remember at fifteen years old being anxious about going to this wonderful place my friends kept bragging about. It was summertime. You could tell by how green the grass and leaves were. Not to mention the melting, beaming sun shining down on us. My older brother called me to tell me, "Be ready!" He's 32 years old now, running his own little business in Thornton, Colorado. A busy body is what I like to call him because he never takes a day off. As we approached our destination and walked in...there it was, a bright shiny gold and black AKG microphone. It was the shape of a spray paint can calling my name. Next to it was a run down, rusty silver music stand covered in dust, as if it had been sitting there since the 1800's. The headphones on my ears poured out beautiful music every time my music engineer, a man named Brian, who had a degree in music engineering, pressed the play button. By the look of his clothes, he reminded me of a hippie from the sixties. A laid back 40-year-old man that spoke with a soft calm voice, his feedback was always the same response, "I thought it was cool." The room around me had brown-stained walls as if coffee was brewing and leaking from the ceiling. The room looked old and beat up, similar to a New York subway station. A soundproof window blocked out the interruptions of unwanted sounds trying to make their way from the outside in. On the other side of the window was me, a fifteen-year-old teenager recording the music I desired to create so passionately in this unique small place called The Mouse Trap. The vibe of this room captured our laughs, smiles, tears, and joy like a Kodak camera. It made me, my brother, and my circle of friends feel safe. A place where we were able to be ourselves. We created unforgettable memories at that place, as well as some awesome music. So, excuse me while I get back to what I do best...creating wonderful music!

ANTHONY GILLESPIE

Everyday Street Ties

Born in it, groomed by it, and every day I was surprised by it! The streets may come plural in sense, but they are a single parent, one similar unit, a common denominator, or the babysitter that's always available. One day could be the dead-beat dad that indirectly showed you the way, then the next the magical mom whose best trick was her disappearing act. We all have a deep loving aunt, but really, her misery just needed some company. A wild weekend with an uncle could leave you unknowingly horny, curiously hungover and wondering in confusion, but, ready to do it all over again next weekend. The best of all, Grandma's house, where there are no rules!

Every son naturally looks up to their father like shiny stars in the night sky. Well, mine stayed on a money hustle and juggling women, so in the streets I found shooting stars, a dark-bright moon, and everything else the universe had to offer. Then a mother that didn't know the difference between being here and just being there, I guess she tried, but I didn't stick around to find out. I didn't get a "Good Morning," breakfast and a ride to school. I was lucky if there was a splash of almost-spoiled milk for a half-a-bowl of Cheerios before I kicked rocks all the way to school. There was no Twinkie-yellow school bus. Twenty bucks a month granted you public bus transportation on the R.T.D, better known as the "Raggedy Tour of Denver." Aunties and uncles were merely grown children as they played on with minimal responsibility. All the while Grandma was the captain of the ship, pilot to the plane and driver in the train. So, what she said, goes! For

13 years she was that and more for me, with the streets only having weekend visitation rights. Then her unfortunate departure paved the road to my complete adoption by Mr. & Mrs. Streets!

The streets can take a joyful youth spoiled with innocence, aggressively force adaptation upon them, and immediately fill your résuméwith a wide range of experience. With that adaptation you live and learn, fall, and get back up, struggle but overcome, all to survive and see another day, tomorrow's relative with another life lesson. One day could be 72-hours of no sleep, non-stop grinding and unplanned involvements that finally end only for the next to begin just as fast as a revolving door lets people in and out. "Sleep when you die," and "Tomorrow ain't promised," are just a couple of the unwillingly inherited and, unfortunately, unfair models you live by as you never realize you're simply, "Living to die," while "Dying to live!" But just as the streets can raise you, they can break you, cheat on you, become the untrustworthy not-so-significant other. In one day, take witness to it all—the good, the bad, the ugly!

Growing up in the streets I barely continued from a baby to a child, and never graduated from a child to a teenager. Raised as a young man whose hand-me-downs were family responsibilities and, instead of chores, an actual "9-to-5." School was by choice with no apparent consequences, but the root of all evil was deeply implanted early and the love of money was well established as a priority. The streets can raise you and prepare you like a wise father and loving mother, by strengthening your character, molding values and principles, and developing your true potential. With each day, you have to respect it like an elder! As it's an elder of much experience, just frowned upon because it's viewed upon in a negative light. When really, it's simply tough love when accepted, a tremendous development like none other.

C.J.D.

"Mom, have you been drinking?" You ask her this when you notice her words slurred. "No!!" she laughs, and says she has an appointment with the doctor tomorrow. "Okay, well let me know," you reply. She calls the next day and explains that they're putting her in speech therapy classes and are doing an MRI also. They think it has something to do with the car accident she was in just weeks prior. She asks you to drive her to speech therapy and, while you're waiting, you text a cousin in New York who's dating a renowned neurologist, "Number two in the state," she tells you. The doctors in Colorado aren't finding anything, but you'll feel better with another opinion. You send the MRI off to New York with hopeful results. Two weeks pass and a call arrives. A call that cracks your foundation, weakens your structure and alters your life eternally. "Sit down," she tells you, "I have news and it's not good." She's crying and trying to explain a complicated disease her boyfriend called C.J.D. Her words and doctor terms are unfathomable through crying and her tears. She sums it up by saying "Dennis, you need to prepare, she will begin to decline rapidly!"

"Okay," you say, but your mind is in pure denial. "You need to prepare," she tells you again. Months go by and speech class remains the same, mom's still cooking, cleaning and showing no signs of declining. "That doctor and cousin are full of shit!!" you think to yourself. Then arrives.

Christmas, in the middle of your twelve hour shift you text mom, "When are we making tamales? I'll buy everything but the red chile, because you already have some." Her reply "I can't help you," maybe she misunderstood, so you text her back. She replies, "You don't understand, I can't help you."

Right then at that very moment, everything slows down, stands still, and it all comes smashing down like waves hitting rocks on the eve of a storm. The naps that come more frequently, her blank stares while conversing, her loss of balance concluded with an utterance of unintelligible slurred words. You call the cousin, "Is mom really dying?" She says calmly as if coming to terms with it, "I told you to prepare!" The fact she was so composed sends you into a panic, an uncontrollable sob, filled with rage, grief, sorrow, fury, anguish, agony, hurt and pain. The emotions are endless. The more level-headed the cousin was, the more it sends you into a blizzard of emotions. Now you know C.J.D. is real, and it's very hard to prepare for something you have no skill with. One-in-a-million chance that one will inherit this disease, it's not hereditary or genetic. But you need to prepare as it pokes pin-sized holes in mom's brain, quickly taking away speech and mobility. Prepare because, within two years, she will make her final departure. No amount of love can stop this, there's no treatment or medication. She will leave behind all that you cherish, adore and treasure—leaving her memory. Going away leaving you, as you are still learning to prepare.

LUTHER HAMPSON

Birds

I battle for balance, my legs like stilts, making their way, step-over-step across the fallen log that lay over the swift moving creek. The pack I lug, too large for one night, I had misdeemed when filling it. I was living the pain of not being a minimalist when it came to my outdoor exploits. A maximalist perhaps? Better to have it and not need it then need it and not have it. I never needed it. I'd been primed to start a fire with sticks years before I learned to drive, yet I carried nine alternatives for my desire to incept men's red flower.

As the sun set, unhurried as it descended into the horizon, the resonance of the night began to slowly set in. I flicked my Petzl Duo headlamp into its energy-sourcing LED setting and kept my eyes glued to the earth, yearning for the small treasures I was seeking. Minerals, arrowheads, millennia-old pottery, Spanish coins. Whatever. My eyes combed the ground as my steps lay out a grid, a technique I learned from my time volunteering in the local K-9 Search and Rescue. Hours later, to my chagrin, the only treasure I found was dirt, rocks and trees. Had I been the proprietor of a gravel pit or a sawmill, I'd be in the green, but as circumstances had it on this evening, those commodities were worthless to me. Abandoned the search, I did. Sequestered from the burden of my pack, I lay down on a bed of stones and spent some time silently looking at the sky. Lex Luther, Stargazer.

Down with the scorpions, spiders, and other creatures of the night, a darkness, uncontaminated by the cancer of human habitation, left a lucifugous footprint, perfect for viewing the night sky in the Four

Corners area. I could see clearly the faint light of several satellites as they made their way across the orb that are the heavens, watching "them" watch me.

I commence my search in earnest. Making my way to the top of the mesa, I negotiate an obstacle of sandstone. Near the pinnacle I feel the buzz of an incoming text rattle my device. I reach for my phone as I hang from the cliff, more interested in checking in on my lifeline than keeping my life in check. I take my hand from the hold, letting my other hand, being used as a chock in the vertical crock running along the rockface, bear the weight of me and my behemoth of a pack I carry. I fumble. Fuck! I focus my beam to something shiny a dozen feet below. I finish my climb and untroubled myself from my Osprey Zenith pack before I descend to retrieve my flip phone. Yes, flip phone. Near the bottom, my hand rests on something alien in this landscape. In a world of jagged edges and cactus flesh, what I'm touching now is anything but that. Like some sort of chondrule received from space, sitting in a nearly inaccessible spot in a cliff face in the desert southwest lies what appears to be an egg. More grand than a chicken egg, but not quite the size of an ostrich, this egg was like no other I'd seen. Petrified, I stood, motionless in contemplation over what I just found.

I yell to my partner.

"I think I found a dinosaur egg."

"Yeah right, let me see," he responds.

I see his light slice through the darkness as he makes his way towards my discovery. I finish climbing down, pick up my phone, not bothering to see if it's broken and place it in my pocket, neglecting the text I was so eager, just seconds before, to check. I show him my treasure.

"Son of a bitch," he sighs.

"You lucky motherfucker," he adds.

Looking it over we came to the same conclusion, what I found was indeed an egg. I could find no carton, no "best if used by" date. Having turned to stone, this complete protein, I assume, is at least 65 million years old. A raptor? Just miles from the Utah border, could it be the Utahraptor? Or the more infamous Velociraptor?

Back on the log, my legs feel a little less burdened. The pack, though a little heavier than before, seems to float on my shoulders, perhaps my Osprey has got its wings. I show the landowner and he allows me to be the conservator of my discovery. This outing leaves me with one conclusion: this treasure hunting stuff is, well, what do they say, for the birds.

LYSANDER HARVEY

Change

How long does it take for change? A lifetime, a year, a day, a moment, maybe never? Does an abandonment of an act cause change? Maybe it's unyielding like the child being told to wait to eat the savory-sour-candy. How long?

Tick-tock, tick-tock, have you changed yet? Meditate and you shall change? Will praying to Allah bring you change? Maybe science has the answer? Is it the Bible that must become your idol? The Ten Commandments, must you follow? Only when you ask Jesus can you change? Like a fine-filtered picture, will one be diminished in the former image, or always remembered for such a profound blemish?

What about your mannerism? Must you conduct yourself as those who are beautifully painted in the powerful pen? Has history changed? Can the color of your skin change? Can you have change for your cents? Or is it you only receive change for the all-inclusive-almighty dollar? How long before your account changes? How long has it been? Count the seconds, count the minutes, count the hours. Has it changed?

M A R K   H O R T O N

How Not to House Train a Puppy

"Mom! Zoey pooped in my room again!"

"You know what the puppy training expert said to do. Pick Zoey up, then rub his face into the mess he made. Being sure to stress how disappointed you are in him, and how much of a 'BAD DOG' he is, otherwise he'll never learn his lesson."

*

"Bad dog Zoey! Look at this mess you made; you are a bad, bad boy! No! No more messes in the house! When you mess in the house you hurt me! Why do you want to hurt me, Zoey? Just look at the mess you made! BAD DOG!"

*

Would you believe that Zoey was never house trained? Even though everyone in my family rubbed his cute little Ewok face into every pile of shit, puddle of piss, and destroyed property. Zoey never learned. Even though we were his loving family that knew best, we never stopped and realized that Zoey's messes were just an outward sign of an inward problem. We never paused in our day to notice the early warning signs that Zoey was in turmoil. We never paid attention to his distress. We never thought, "Maybe we should spend more time with Zoey outside." We never connected his anxiety to the mess he made.

Boy oh boy, do I ever identify with Zoey now that I'm in recovery and incarcerated. I wake up every day having my face rubbed into the mess I made: "Bad boy! Bad dog!—Look at what you did!—How dare you lie to me?!—I can't believe the choices you made!—Bad boy!—Look at this mess! You did this! Bad boy!"

I wonder if Zoey ever lays in his bed at night wondering how his family was so blind to his distress, so deaf to his cries for "Help!" so out of touch with what he was going through. I wonder if his last thought each night was that "I don't want to be a bad dog, I want to be a Good Boy."

DAVID IRONS

Persona, Personify, Person

Whether it's accurate or not, what someone believes of themselves tends to manifest in their character, personality, and behavior. In my case, for most of my life, I lived out a persona. A persona is defined as being "an individual's social façade or front." I lived in this manner, believing I was required to somehow be the kind of person others wanted me to be.

For example, as a kid my mom knew I loved sports and music. To encourage me in this, she bought me footballs, baseballs, and other sports related stuff. She also engaged in piano lessons with me. However, even though I enjoy these activities, within me, I didn't feel like these things would become a larger, more permanent part of my life. I just wasn't sure being a football player or musician was any part of who I am as a person.

Then as a teenager, I landed my first job at a Burger King. I loved it! Making food and serving people felt like a natural fit. I loved this kind of work so much I pursued jobs at as many restaurants as I could: Casa Bonita, Old Spaghetti Factory, even IHOP, it didn't matter. At this point I believe I had arrived at being personified. I felt a greater sense of purpose, but not quite self-actualized. In context, I was an abstract person.

Then, one day, while visiting my grandfather, he asked, "Do you ever think you'll amount to much?" At first, I wasn't sure what he meant. I was too stumped to even ask. A few years after he posed that question, he died without my answer. Overall, his question has taken a large portion of 50 years to even reach an answer.

In contemplating his question, in light of how he loved me, I realized that his question was an enigma. I took his question and rephrased it, "Do you understand how valuable you are?" Doing this helped me understand that as an individual I am valued for being who I am and doing what I love. That is, of course, if what I love doing is of benefit to myself as well as others. As a result, his words have driven me to discover, it's okay to be me.

Unique

Falling, always falling, my essence gathers, until, in one glorious instant I become whole, unique, a snowflake drifting upon the wind. Uncounted millions of my brothers and sisters fall all around me, each just as unique as I. Some, like me, are content to drift while others band together falling heavier and faster through the sky.

With each passing moment of my existence, my being changes, never the same from one second to the next. My crystals grow in complexity, sometimes growing long and beautiful, sometimes squat and malapropos. Regardless, it is change and ties into the whole. What will I be when my falling comes to an end, I wonder?

The wind shifts and I catch an updraft spinning me higher into the sky. Looking down I see that some of my fellows weren't so fortunate and are slammed to the ground quickly. Why was I spared that same fate? Bewildered by the experience, I move on, continuing to drift, always changing into a more and more complex pattern.

Looking closely at the beauty of one snowflake as it comes close, I think, "That! I wish I could become like that!" As it drifts farther and farther away on its own course to the ground, I begin pulling moisture to me. To some degree I shape myself into the beauty of the other, but I am unable to change what has already taken shape, only that which grows after.

As I continue to fall, I'm left with a choice. Do I cover up my scars under layer upon layer or do I leave them free to face the night air and grow out from there? Already I am unique amongst the endless hordes of other snowflakes, for my journey to the ground is my own.

For a time, I'm persuaded one way, then another, almost as fickle as the wind itself. Always bumping into other snowflakes on our fall, who, for that brief contact, influence how I fall and how I grow. Even as the ground comes nearer and my form more fixed, I wonder if others will see my unique beauty or just a pile of snow. Or, is it as I fear, my scars all too visible to the naked night that I will melt before the final rest, my beauty lost, never to be seen?

DERRICK MILLER

Crash-Landing Before Takeoff

By the age of six, I already had the beginnings of a personal myth. Uninformed, unsophisticated, undeniably present. A Leo born at the Air Force Academy, I knew enough to understand lions were kings and the Air Force ruled the sky—in some mysterious but obvious way, I partook of this.

That year, for my birthday or Christmas, from which of my grandparents I don't recall, I was gifted with the coolest toy ever. A fighter jet, made for G.I. Joe, who was awesome in his own right. Even better, it was an F-14 with its back-swept wings and predatory stance. The Tomcat. A feline raptor. As such, it was the embodiment of power, joy, pride, protection, fierceness. Just not in so many words. Here was my personal totem. Or so I would have named it if I had the ability.

One day, through sheer coltish clumsiness, I knocked down one of my mother's collected clocks. It was fine mechanically; not so cosmetically. A small thing. A simple thing. I was devastated nonetheless. Unfortunately, mom wasn't home. Her husband was. This worthy witness decided I needed a lesson. Carrying my plane in one hand, dragging me with the other, we made the querulous trek to the garage. Throwing my jet to the ground upon arrival, precious pieces I had taken such care with snapped off, careening in too many directions to follow. The light tinkling of skipping, skating plastic—the loudest sound in the world. Screaming, ranting and raving about destroying another's property, this vengeful titan took up a bat. Smash. Deeming the action insufficient, I was forced to take a couple of swings for good measure.

As I sat there staring at, crying over, my ruined plane, I made a new discovery: hate. Despair. Fear. Regret. Dismay. Betrayal. There were no words for these. They were utterly foreign, but oh, so powerful.

Years later, my mother asked why I never said anything. What was there to say? It was a toy plane. How was I to know I had bound too much into plastic, or that its destruction hopelessly tangled so many new, overwhelming emotions into an effective Gordian knot?

Today, while I lament the loss of innocence that day, a crash landing before takeoff, there is a sense of gratitude. From the landfill, the ghost of my childish totem still speaks. A hidden treasure formed of bedrock ideals, immaterial and indestructible, it reminds me of all I have overcome, all I have become. It reminds me no demigod can stop me from soaring high, flying free, or pursuing my ambitions with the pride, joy, power of a winged lion. And this isn't such a bad thing at all.

Words

A dictionary can one day rival an armored tank. It can be a submarine missile shot at 1000 miles per hour. It can be a spaceship moving at the speed of light. Words represent images and symbols. To some people words are powerful, they kill more people than guns, they move mountains, they shape the world as we know it. They change the world's future, they explain the world's past. They get you into trouble, they get you out of trouble. They explain how to do things and work, they build rockets that go to outer space, they give you information, they convey emotions. They inspire people, they excite people, they make you smile, they make you angry, and it's not just limited to people. Animals communicate also. The birds chirp, the lions roar, the dogs bark, the cats meow. Words are the most powerful weapon I've ever seen, heard, or had. When I cried and screamed as a baby, I commanded adults with my vocal cords. Imagine a world where nobody made any noise whatsoever. No music, no laughing, no arguing, no whistles, no bells, no cars honking, no lightning storms, no football crowds screaming at the top of their lungs for defense, no communication whatsoever. Even if you're deaf, sign language is key for survival. I love my words. That is why I choose them carefully. Words can be flexible, you can tell any story you want. You can say anything you want. Your mouth is the one thing that nobody else can control. It is yours and you can use it how you see fit. You can make anything in the universe with words and a dictionary is like an armored chest.

T E R R E N C E   R I C H A R D S O N

A Kansas City Chiefs Blanket

A Kansas City Chiefs blanket: red and yellow, soft and lush, comfortable and rough, loving and kind, relatable and encouraging, my friend in dark places my family would go. My Kansas City Chiefs blanket was the only memory my dad left me, so I carried it everywhere. My Chiefs blanket was my hope when I was bloody, unrecognizable and couldn't speak. The blanket represented the security, love, and happiness I felt I would never receive. My Kansas City Chiefs blanket was everything I needed in a very vulnerable, desperate and desolate time. As I became a teenager, no longer was the blanket huge to my frame, it seemed as if I made the blanket normal to the extent of personification. No longer was the blanket a sense of security because I learned things that happen are destined from birth, but my blanket still reminded me of the love I so desperately wanted and needed; it was worn, comfortable and still smelled of smoke as my blanket miraculously survived a house fire the year I turned nine. Smelling the smoke on the blanket was a release since I was incarcerated, surrounded by white walls, locked doors, and linoleum floors. As a child being incarcerated just because your parents don't want you and you misbehave for attention, it's rough, so smelling freedom was my only escape. Once again the Kansas City Chiefs blanket provided me with coping mechanisms necessary to surviving unfortunate events demoralizing only in essence that I felt hopeless. But the hope of my father returning, however weak it was, lived on through that Kansas City Chiefs blanket until he was killed, my father shot down in Kansas City, Missouri, and I couldn't look at that blanket anymore. He lied to me, my father who loves me, lied to me, his son. So the blanket had to burn as it did into ash, just like daddy.

JAROD ROBERTSON

Love is the Epitome of Flash Nonfiction

Ashlee loved Mark's card, she loved orchids, she loved her darling of a sister, Destiny. Ashlee was troubled, yet terrific. She loved music and contemporary art. She was radiant, yet reticent. She was a giver of light, yet she was consumed by darkness. Ashlee was an enigma. She was also an important part of my nonfiction: Experienced, Yet Gone in a Flash.

The joyous way she gazed in my longing eyes sent shockwaves through my core every morning after bed checks and med call. The electrical charge she sent through the circuitry of me was indisputably felt and conveyed. Our forbidden forays and restricted rendezvous on the periphery of the cameras and caseworkers always produced a ruddiness to her fair features which I found to further foment a ferocity of feelings and fulfillment.

The flash nonfiction of lovebirds languishing in the lockdown of a mental institution: loony from life, yet levitating because of this loony love.

The ease in which our energies intertwined; our auras commingling made it abundantly clear that our coexistence, coupled with a copious amount of contemplation of copulation, created a current of uncorrupted caring—mightier than the Colorado River coursing through the crevices of canyons. Love and affection. A care that couldn't be contained. A rose that arose from the cracks to grow unconsciously in the crater of medicated consciousness.

A love that couldn't be confined even within the confines of a convent for the crazies!

One flew over the cuckoo's nest and caught a glimpse of a peacock. And although this peacock didn't possess the perfect plumes, this crow's courtship nonetheless was commenced and complete.

A crazy love in a crazy place.

"Have you taken your medicine today?" I ask, "Your aura is opaque and your energy misplaced."

"But your love is my drug," She replies, with a smile that radiates through her cinnamon eyes.

A straitjacket love encircling my being, enveloping in a straitjacket environment.

Ashlee—my peacock, my patient, my nurse practitioner! My . . . psychiatrist?

Like flash nonfiction was our love and your life—or better yet, just your life, because our love is everlasting. Romeo and Juliet-esque, frozen in time.

Was it my banishment and sudden departure that elicited your ingestion of elixir? The revocation of our reverie reverberates in my mind, making me wonder if our rupturing ramped up your retrogression—each subsequent slash to your smooth skin symbolic.

Just the other day my friend was watching the movie *Anger Management*, and the moment I saw Jack Nicholson, I couldn't help but reminisce about the time when this old crow flew over the cuckoo's nest and caught a glimpse of the most perfect peacock with imperfect plumes.

ADAM STARK

The Marks We Make

Pencil plus paper equals lines. It's a complication of simple math. Adding a pencil to the paper and creating lines. Written or drawn, doesn't matter; straight or curved, when, where or how. In the end, only the lines count.

Lines are our self-expressions. The painted walls that separate us from other people. It can be a cure without an analysis, an identity, or a fingerprint, these marks we make. They can show the world the real us, the line in the sand that says, "Here, and yet, so much further." A window between the heart and mind, hinting at the soul that is.

In hundreds, even thousands, of years from now, when we are all gone and all that remains is paper with lines on it—those lines, those shapes that tell a picture, that draw a story—will be what those who come after learn of us. Those pages bearing the marks we leave are a legacy for our children and theirs.

From the most ancient and most hard won finger paintings on the cave walls, to tomorrow's fastest and lightest keystrokes, to make a mark is to be human. These lines are physical representations, non-verbal communication of ideas. There are not a lot of creatures in the world that can do this. Bears, for example, will scratch trees to mark their territory and so do we humans. Only our trees are processed into paper, and we scratch away with pens and pencils instead of claws, but the concept is the same.

They shape this world, the marks we make. Horrendous, beautiful or dull. Both artistic expression and literary form show who the artist is becoming, not who they are. No matter the shapes used = they show the force behind the form. To build inspirations that can last through the ages and draw lines that never end. The forms of the lines are unimportant without the forces that shape them. One is useless without the other.

It's just simple math, but it can also be so much more, has to be more. At least, it should be more. They can be disgusting or lovely, confusing or confident, enjoyable or scary. It is what it is, but without the heart and mind, without the soul, it won't be what it can be. Put force into the forms, because in the end, only the lines count.

Rule of Thumb

The first time I ever hitchhiked was around eight years old. We had recently moved to a new apartment complex and one afternoon while out exploring, I got lost. It was frightening.

Giving some approximation of the easily recognizable hitchhiker "mudra"—arm extended, thumb up, I flagged down what turned out to be a cop, who stopped to see what the hell I was doing. I told him the problem and we managed to get me back home, maybe three blocks away at that point. Now, this will stand out as perhaps the only time a meeting with the police turned out favorably. I'll give credit where it's due.

From the age of twelve or so, it wasn't unusual for me to thumb rides around town. Fairly quickly, you learned to spot the creepy ones, usually overweight, balding, and nervous, asking weirdo shit like "So, you got a girlfriend, sport?" From there, you knew it wouldn't be long before the old hand-on-the-thigh move. "Um, yeah. Here's where I get out." Revolting. It was typical behavior for me at the time to be drunk or on downers or weed. Did I realize how risky that behavior was? Yep. Back then I was fearless and occasionally violent. It could have turned out badly, I realize.

My brother was also a hitcher and he went all over the states. We both had the rambling gene, I guess. As souvenirs, he would save the cellophanes off his cigarette packets, each having the states' different tax stamps on the bottom.

My longest haul was in October of 1990—San Francisco, California, to Richmond, Virginia. 3000 miles. I was living in the coastal northern California town of Eureka for about a year and decided to go back to the East Coast. First I had business down in the Bay Area and friends to see. My last weekend was spent in Bolinas, in the city, and a day trip down to Santa Cruz. After having my fill of the city and many farewell libations with my friends, I got on a local bus to Marin City, stopping long enough to acquire some of the herbal refreshment Northern Cali is so justifiably famous for. Thus fortified, I began hitching east.

Almost immediately, I ran up on a snag. Some kid that picked me up took me to Petaluma, like 60 miles out of my way. That night was spent under an overpass, cold and pissed off, waiting for the morning light so I could get my bearings. Plan B was to go up through Sacramento and that's what happened. On the on-ramp in Sac, I was ousted by the CHP. They told me I better act right. Moving on, we sailed into Winnemucca in a Winnebago, there dropped by the dusty road and so, into Nevada. That night to drift, dreamily, through the desert starscape. I may have seen a UFO but can't be certain. Your mind can play tricks alone in the desert at night.

The day eventually dawned, like an irrational hope, on morning sky washed, arid terrain. I was heartily glad when a small silver-blue truck pulled over to pick me up. The driver motioned to get in the back so my faded blue canvas duffle bag and I hopped in. There to remain for most of two days and 1,000 miles of open Western country. Head down, suffering silently, through cold rain and sleet as the urine-esque, beachy brown of the Utah salt flats wafted by, cold and dead. Jim, the driver, let me crash the floor of his hotel at night and I was grateful.

When we came to Iowa, we parted company. Jim heading on and over to New York and I making my way southeast, eager to avoid the urban bullshit of New York City, Newark, Philadelphia, Baltimore, Washington D.C., and the northeast gauntlet of I-95.

Midafternoon, St. Louis, Missouri, I stop and have some draft beers at the bar of a corporate hotel you will have heard of. My spirits lift, I pick my way across the dicey, decaying catwalks of overpass and railway bridge in East St. Lou, finally onto the bridge across and above The

Big Muddy. The Mississippi River, majestic and filthy, wide of wash, earth becomes water. And so, eastward through bombed-out looking industrial hinterlands. Made my way down into Southern Illinois and by now I'm starting to "feel the burn," you could say. Moving is the easy part.

By the side of the road, thumb out, a tractor-trailer tumbles into view, brakes locking, shuddering to a stop on the shoulder. Passenger door swings open. I climb up and in after giving the driver the obligatory once-over. He appears pleased with himself. He's got an open fifth of whiskey in between his legs, half empty. I am, er, apprehensive but a ride's a ride so, onward. For a few miles and suddenly he pulls over to the side of the road and says "Hey, you wanna drive?" before passing out cold. I politely decline and exit the truck as it sits idling and walk on.

Over into Kentucky, I'm picked up by a guy named Larry in a compact white station wagon. He tells me he transports school busses from his home in North Carolina to Southern California; I've caught him on the return trip. Really nice guy. In fact, I have met many totally cool, kind-hearted people while hitching and during the time I spent living on the street. I call them angels. They have allowed me to hold onto a little bit of hope for the human race. Larry got me into the mountains of West Virginia and the last leg of this jaunt.

At a dead stop, my head and body humming with exhaustion. I spend the entire night sitting on my duffle bag beside the on-ramp, somewhere in those god-forsaken mountains. Maybe five cars go by the whole night, none stop. At some point I began hearing disembodied music, jazz, emanating from an indiscernible source. The rock cliffs off to my right begin to shimmer, then shimmy, and finally morph into what looks like the "California Raisins" and proceed to dance in a sort of conga line. I realize I am badly sleep deprived. The night got weirder and swung through an elastic arc falling towards daybreak.

I awake in full sunlight. Must have dozed off briefly. Coming to, feeling somewhat sorted out and refreshed. A very dapper-looking, bright-eyed older fellow pulls up in a Volkswagen Beetle. Gives me half his breakfast of coffee and bagel with cream cheese. A gesture that is touching in its civility and human-ness. Almost surreal in its normalcy. The driver happens to be a school teacher and he gets me to Afton Mountain, Charlottesville, Virginia. Sunday morning. Now I'm 60 miles from home!

The final ride on that run was from a group of three or four young dudes headed up to D.C. for a concert. We are all in a happy, upbeat mood. We pass around a pint bottle of bourbon and some herb to celebrate being alive, young, and free. The sun shines its radiance on the trees beside the highway. The leaves sizzle and pop—red, yellow, orange. Decked out in their October Shenandoah best.

On reaching my destination, I eat half a large cheese pizza and sleep like a burnt out baby for two days.

ANTHONY RAY VALDEZ

Traveling Beat Junkie

The lowest bass tone afforded me a glimpse in my rearview. When the next beat dropped to an 808, the Rocky Mountains' slopes danced into a blur of greens, reds and tan highlights. My 1973 Pontiac Grand Prix traveled more than roads—carrying a spirit from voyages between proprietors of family and friends—Chris's dad, Chris, Phil, then to me, I felt the independence each man before me must have felt on an open highway.

The song's break commenced into beautiful soft vocals as Sierra Leone flirtatiously liberated the tweeters. This was my first time moving out of Colorado on my own. Going to the unknown with certainty my hopes would flourish. A momentary halt of bass brought my mirrors to a standstill where I saw my bleached tips above my tan visor hat, a babyface with the surest of eyes reflected back. My most normal vanity, with a kiss and a wink, ignited a blitzkrieg of conviction with Mt. Eden's crescendo.

This stretch of I-70 resonated nostalgic familiarity with unacquainted responsibilities. Vibrating formless shapes on my driver's door mirror replicated my internal assessment of self. The mirror's stationary and strong housing was the brawn harboring reflections of the past. My past, rattling and still intermittently with parts of Sierra Leone, left my soul touched. Every element aligned, telling me my sudden departure from all I've known and loved was the next step in life.

A smirk, common on my lips when I realized the gravity of my actions, appeared as the wind from the sunroof brushed my hair. I felt at ease while asphalt lines directed me around curves seeming to coexist with each step of my favorite song.

Sierra Leone was looped perpetually; January's chilled mountain air held the vocalist's notes in a way that made me feel resiled. Embarking on this journey was a haste decision . . . no plans—no resources—no home—no idea what the hell I was getting myself into. The winter's sunshine played dazily on the deep-purple tinted windows as I ventured west, following the road like sheet music. Composure and melancholy filled my ambitions; everything behind is now gone. Inevitability of growth fueled this journey. I know not what came next except the larkiness felt from the music's aura.

All my fears lulled by the softness of her voice making me oblivious to any unease. Her melodic tone laced over the beats silenced the unsettlement of my thoughts. A glare in the stillness as the low hum emitted, my reflection met me with confidence telling me to lead with my heart as my foot pressed the accelerator.

ETHAN VIRGIL

On the Run

The beginning of an end. On a highway that resembles obsession. El finally Vegas; choice of route: colorful I-70. Ford wheels skitter, winter land highway. Two steps left, the hatchbacks' driver-side door is a cliff face, a right arm from rocky Colorado's whitewashed mountain.

Your music selection resembles how you feel.

"You used to be my brother . . ." Drums thump to eardrum, creating a sonic wonderland. Keef smoke sparks at my face. I'm holding the top shelf hostage from my wife in the driver seat. She's navigating and I'm stowed human cargo. I succumb to my own universe leaving white noise.

An antagonist versus an antihero in my antebellum neighborhood where I lost it, all tryna win. Yellow tape duel. Old friend crack ricochets the air. Predators slither in silence to violence . . . or to seize another day.

Blow clouds. Vision impaired, a woman, not my wife, at the wheel. Moment screwed, present sun at high noon, to her return pilgrimage, alone devastated, clothes knock around the car. Marital roles at an infant responsibility. I'm pissing away.

Sometimes you feel the music to match.

"But you stabbed me in the back . . . and I had to double back." Revenge, return the damage. Break the sky. Zero life repossessed. Pent up emotions exhausted. I had to double back.

The part of the chorus that's playing in your head.

"You used to sleep on the floor in my momma's house, so when

I see you . . . I'ma air you out. If I see you in a crowd I'ma stare you down . . ."

On this highway: a spiritual race, a higher power plan. The most surreal pat before intermission, re-cap, re-hash, then cease the spinning mercury. Attached to thin string as a copper penny twirls. Who is he to intercede with him except with his permission he knows what happens to them in this world and the hereafter. On the run, please respond.

La Vista
Correctional Facility

LORAINE ABEYTA

Voice of Experience

From sticks to stone, I'd moved from a small midwestern mountain town to the outskirts of Los Angeles, California. It wasn't just culture shock; it was chaos. A new arrival to Florence Nightingale Middle School, I watched in amazement as students piled off city busses instead of school busses and I wondered why there was no grass or curb appeal. Stained and weathered concrete lay in every direction, pausing only to make way for battered blacktop and occasional clouded puddles of water. The unrepaired cracks and chips should have been a red flag, a warning of what was ahead, a hint to the generation ignored and neglected beyond the gates.

High chain link fences enclosed the entire city block making the entrance difficult to find. My palms were sweaty, and my overstuffed backpack was knocking me off balance as I paced behind a line of brunettes who appeared to know their way. Where were all the blondes?

A chilling giant, Nightingale was a monster—dark and dreary, decades old, intimidating and at least seven times the size of my colored school. A compound really only to compare to what I'd know of concentration camps in grade school studies of *Mein Kampf*. There was one large main building with crowded rows of portable, temporary buildings behind it. I'd later discover them to be used as classrooms.

Oversized steel and brass double doors seemed to laugh at me as I entered to find a set of metal detectors I'd pass through next. Why did seventh graders need to be metal detected? Oppression hung hazily in the air. A skunky aroma wafted across my face which I recognized as marijuana. I'd first encountered it on a camping trip with my parents and stepdad's college buddies. This unwelcome intruder would become very familiar to me over the months that followed.

Marijuana would soon fog my thinking, numb my pain and satisfying my appetite for mischief. I grew to embrace the foul-smelling miracle plant and would eventually find myself alongside my peers on the east corner of the grounds puffing and passing the makeshift pipe, a horizontally held soda can. These twelve-year-olds were innovative. What a strange place I was in.

Spanish and Chinese were the dominant languages confusing my ears as I listened for English to absorb. Breakfast sloshed around in my stomach, nervously bubbling its way back up my throat. The bell whined and a vigorous wave of white polos and navy-blue pants crashed through the halls as tweens reluctantly escaped each other's embraces and spilled into hallway openings. Swept away by the currents I eventually found my way.

Overwhelmed and defeated I stumbled into science class with a half dozen others. We were all several minutes late but Mr. Dam was consumed by a novel that was enough to earn a passing grade at Florence Nightingale.

Worthy

All my life I had thought I was unworthy of God's love.

However, God loves me unconditionally regardless of what I believe or think.

As time goes by, this beautiful song keeps reassuring me that God loves me! I have learned throughout the years that life isn't in any way easy! Life is so interesting because you can believe what you want, but the truth is that we find ourselves when we pray and believe.

It's not until then that our life makes any sense.

Now that I've processed these feelings and emotions, I can fully understand that no matter what, my father God loves me and I don't have to do anything to deserve it.

We however, at times, take his love for granted or ignore it. I have accepted the fact that I do have to be good to people. I have to forgive in order to be forgiven. In this world, I can do anything I set my mind to, as long as I put in effort and grab God by His hand.

In order for me to succeed, I first have to fail. But I also realize that failure, trials and tribulations will give me spiritual and mental growth.

Therefore, I will strive to be better and reach my goals . . .

SARAH BEAUDOIN

Out My Window

Raindrops fall gently on my window pane. They slide slowly, carelessly down to collect in pools flooding the edge opposite of the glass. I stand on the inside of the curtain as if it could transport me away from this place. Daydreaming that this window has the ability to take me out of here and into a better world. Somewhere violence doesn't exist. Where people want to be kind and loving. I stand on my toes and press my forehead against cold glass. I close my eyes and my fingers cling to the white painted windowsill. The door crashes open and my mother begins to yell, pulling me back into the reality I endure. I turn around quickly as my breathing increases. She expresses her anger for the words I wrote about her in my diary. No place is SAFE. I stand trembling and crying as she storms out of the room, slamming the door behind her. I turn back to my window where the rain has gained momentum. It is beating against my window pain as I sob. Over the years, my window has remained my retreat. Hours are spent here trying to figure out how to get beyond it and into a world I know has to exist. Beyond the world I grew up in, the world I now live in. Days when sunbeams would shine through the glass, reflecting the light, were my favorite. It seemed magical behind my curtain. I could feel the heat like loving arms hugging me. This is the world I long for. Now, in prison, I still do the same thing. People catch me looking out my window, into the beyond for that world of better times. This is where inspiration meets creator. Life of a different kind is formed through imagination. The pain becoming a vehicle for growth and healing as life marches forward.

S T E P H A N I E   D E V E R I C K

Adults Only—
Dusty Dirty Garage

Illinois, in the back of an apartment building sat a dusty dirty garage where so many different things were stored. Seasonal holiday boxes I never wanted to help my mom with! Going through those boxes were like a treasure hunt, hitting the jackpot when finding something we were seeking. This is where my dad spent most of his time after work. He would be out there for hours working, on that rusty old car, that to him was beautiful.

In this garage there were so many tools, that in my youth I didn't really know the names of any of them. They were my dad's pride and joy, Craftsman—best tool known to man. In the right hands, you can make trash into treasure. You could never go wrong with getting him any tool for Christmas or his birthday. If he already had one, it was fine. I remember the first time I saw this car. It was the day that we almost didn't make it home from the used car lot. That car was such a piece of crap, unlike my beautiful bike. Being a kid in a garage like that, nothing felt like mine other than my bike. Everything else was my mom and dad's.

I mean amongst all the boxes were some of my stuff. Like a Christmas stocking, some homemade Christmas stuff that I made at school for my mom. A pile of cans, in the corner in a trash bag was mine. I would go around the block and collect cans for money. That was the greatest thing to do back then when I was maybe ten, if that. I remember the hours my dad spent in that garage with that car and all the nasty gross spots on the ground from that car. The smell in that garage was like no other.

To me just a small kid, that garage was scary for many reasons. There was just so much going on in there. I never wanted to go looking for anything other than getting my bike out or watching my dad work on that car. I never would go into that garage. Watching my dad work on that car was the best thing to look at in that garage. He got so much done to that car. It was becoming a nice looking car, just needed a paint job. I do believe it was a Camaro. That souped up Camaro, went from a dud to a stud. My little brother even called it "Mommy Blue."

Everything

"Dying sun burns in the night
I watch it glow and it's so hard for me"
Every sunset reminds me of him and while I try to find solace in knowing the same sun sets and the same moon rises, the pain is still very real. He is the love of my life, my soulmate, my partner yet miles hold us apart. How can I be complete without him?
"Speaking darkness out of spite
Coercion and then cawing in
Wrap me in bitterness"
It's so easy to get lost in the soft verbiage of injustice in here, but we can either become better or bitter. The choices fall on our own ears—what is my truth? I feel the loss, the humiliating sense of no control. I cause my own suffering because I cannot hold back from wanting him.
"Give it up, I'm complacent
Just enough to escape it
Heretics wouldn't phase me
Lucid trust, I don't want it"
The feelings came in waves and the only way to deal is to compartmentalize them and save the pain for later when I can be alone with my tears and my thoughts. He never leaves my mind. I never expected to find love behind walls and razor wire. I was destined to be what I was told I was: a criminal—less than worthy according to society.
"Palms are rough when you're honest

His hand to lose and wonder why
Your pressure in increments
Like a slow moving coup"

Light words off of a dark cell wall, a candle in no man's land. Love found but yet still lost over the strings of time. Distance means nothing when someone means everything?

"Memories dissident when I am holding you"

If I could only hold him once, I know I could sleep soundly, but then again would it ever be enough? He is my foundation when everything falls apart. When I am misunderstanding, he catches me. He is everything.

TIFFANY GANN

Friends and Hypocrites

Alcoholic:

My father's best friend had been his buddy, Beer. The two were seldomly found apart. My father's love for Beer was much more passionate than that of any of his love affairs. Beer had always been my father's priority.

He woke up with Beer lying by his side, awaiting to be opened for that first satisfying sip, like a good morning kiss touching his lips. Like any good right-hand man, Beer accompanied my father everywhere he went: work, shopping, fishing, special events, everywhere. My father had been a full-blown alcoholic long before my life began and continued to be for the many years to come. His love for alcohol has been greater than the love for himself, his family, for anyone. His alcoholism along with his addiction ultimately lead to his death.

Addiction:

Perhaps my addiction was introduced to me at a young, sensitive age as I observed my father, stepmom and their friends, Beer and Cocaine, constantly partying. They made it look so cool. My childlike mind wanted to imitate my dad. As I became a teenager I was of "drinking age," therefore was now invited to play the game "quarters" with dad and my stepmom. My stepmom had even begun to do lines of cocaine with us during summer vacations. Soon Beer and Cocaine became good friends of mine. Friends I wanted to spend more and more time with. Friends whom, as time passed, I couldn't get away from. Friends who haunted me. Friends whom I now know as addiction.

Hypocrite:

At some point in my father's life, he has made the decision to completely disown and write me out of his life. Erased me as if I never existed. I spent many years resenting my father. I had been torn apart, hurt, and pained by his actions. My father's hateful ways tortured me for far too long. I'd lose sleep wondering what it was I did so horribly wrong that he'd no longer speak to me, no longer acknowledge me being his child, and went so far as to tell my mother, "Tell everyone but Tiffany that I love them." When my uncle had passed and he was sending his condolences, I then realized my father was a hypocrite. All he despised about me, had been the very things he despised of himself. He had been an alcoholic and addict, as was I. He, a terrible father who gave up on his children. I, a mother who spent the majority of her children's adolescent years in and out of prison. Hypocritical my father was. Hypocritical.

K I M B E R L Y   H A R L A N

Gratification

One blissful, sunny, Christmas morning, unlike other Christmas mornings, I awoke with a single purpose. See, in my young life I shared my growing up with three other siblings. Hand-me-downs and being the middle child, I often felt lonely and unable to express myself with words.

Laying in my cozy, toasty waterbed, I would usually fight myself to get up. I was eager to start my morning. Rising up to feel the shaggy carpet under my feet, I made my way down the hallway to the kitchen.

So let me back this story up a bit to the night before to Christmas Eve, which usually was spent with extended family. Much food and spirits to go around. One thing to know about my father was he spared no expense to make holidays special with family. Sometimes to the extent of later repercussions of money not present to pay bills. A generation passed down that I myself inherited and with some of the same consequences in my family with my own kids and husband.

This story has a more sentimental meaning and value in that time of my life. This story is not about just a Christmas story, but about the depth of how one gift really made me feel loved and a close bond to my father whom I looked up to.

As I stepped to the foot of my bed, I noticed the shiny, glimmery, bright light outside my bedroom window. A three-pane window which always woke me up in the morning whether I wanted to rise or not. Browsing my own surroundings I started off down the hallway. "Mmm . . . " I smell bacon and mysterious smells coming from the kitchen. My mom was at the stove cooking bacon. "Eggs, how would you like them?" she asks. Family togetherness as I comprehend the morning, I look outside.

Snowflakes outside shiny, bright, falling from above. Each and every one with a purpose. Each shaped differently. Each size varied. They land on the ground with a beautiful purpose from the heavens they pile together like a mountain of fun and adventure for us kids to enjoy. They melt with every touch.

Catching my attention again to the breakfast at hand, my memory of times in the past where food was a single simple thing that bonded us together.

My brain takes the smells in and my growling tummy yearns in excitement to fill it up. So young, but I understand food equals contentment.

And like a bomb going off in my brain, I realize that the night before Christmas Eve, I did something that will change me for a long time to come. The night before, under the darkness of the hallway, I crept up the dark narrow path and saw an array of lights in the near distance. So off I went, pitter-patter. I arrived in the family room and saw the most beautiful green, blue, yellow, red colors glowing and shining off the walls.

Now some might call it a Christmas tree which, yes, it was. I call it a Christmas Fluffy Package Keeper. A babysitter of surprises to stand and wait for all of us to see what's in them. Instant gratification. So here's where my story gets moral value for me that will impact me for most of my young life.

I am so intrigued by my curiosity that I grab my package to be nosy. I asked this year for a pair of boots. My own boots, no hand-me-downs. My very own, no one else's. I can't wait to see if I get them in the morning.

A little insight into my life. Patience is a virtue I do not hold. In my family, instant gratification comes as a curse for all of us. Money was a root of evil that has in some form come at a great cost to all of us. My dad alone had struggles all our childhood with money problems.

Often gifts, groceries and weekend camping trips came before bills to be paid.

Guilt was an emotion often felt, but no one quite knowing how to process it. I moved on to something distracting. So when opening my present, I felt shame and guilt. I quickly stuffed it away. Looking around I told myself, "Quiet, someone will hear!"

Oh no! What have I done? Starting to cry I felt bad and instantly felt that my happiness had drained. What did I do? I took the surprise away from my mom and dad. The thoughtful gift to me and I stole the surprise as if it was wrapped under the tree as well. The little things matter in life. Later in years, I realized that I thought I didn't deserve this gift.

Getting something expensive that my siblings didn't get made me feel loved. I guess getting something new and spoiling it was a self realization that me wanting things instantly in my life would cause later problems for me.

Consequences for my actions were not something that was handed down to me as much as it was my siblings. Getting away with things was an encouragement to do it again. Later in my life, I carried that trait into my crime of money. My mother stepped away and so did my siblings. In hindsight, I wish consequences would have been greater at a young age to show me limits and boundaries helpful to my success.

SARA LUCAS

Eight Minutes

1, 2, 3, 4, 5, 6, 7, 8. Eight minutes dominated the global news scene. 480 seconds changed the shape of the world! In our fast paced society, eight minutes is a minuscule amount of time that often goes unnoticed. The amount of time it takes to read and respond to an email or the amount of time spent on hold waiting for a customer service representative to take our call. Also, the amount of time it took for a man's life to be choked out! Eight minutes often go unnoticed but, in 2020, eight minutes became the catalyst for change. Eight minutes is not so minuscule when you are the one gasping for air because a police officer has his knee on your neck, applying pressure, cutting off your airway. 480 seconds made Mr. George Floyd a martyr, whether willing or not, for the cause of racial equality, that made the world take notice. The same eight minutes that resonated and sparked protest around the globe. The same eight minutes that paved the way for rich and poor to lock arms and march around the world, shining a light on the plight of the disenfranchised of America. The disenfranchised finally have a voice loud enough to be heard in corporate America and all around the world. In my fifty-two years of life, I've lived in a predominantly non-ethnic, upper middle class neighborhood. Few can understand what being person of color, in that environment, consists of. From being followed through the mall by security, to dealing with school yard jokes or being aware of the intrinsic fear that lies just below the surface of your peers and their families. No matter how educated I am, or loving, there was always a fear that I would become violent if things didn't go my way! Then it happened to my family, yes, racism happened to my upper middle class family. The demoralization and systemic attempt to devalue my family was made painfully obvious when my beautiful son was accused of an atrocious crime, without any evidence, because of the color of his skin. The fact that a case can be brought against him with no legal basis rocked me to my core. I had to face that everything I was raised to believe was a lie. Even if you don't do anything, you need to be aware that you may still have to deal with racism. The responsibility of being the head of my household and role model to my children, I found myself one step away from being emotionally destitute and I could not allow that to happen because there would be no one to guide my children to the place where enlightenment meets healing. In order to prevent them from becoming angry, hostile Black people, I was forced to dig deep and return to my spiritual roots to find a reasonable solution. The combination of the reality of my situation and George Floyd brought me to the understanding that if you are not part of the solution, you are part of the problem. We all have a piece of the solution puzzle, so the question now becomes, will you use your piece or will you bury your head in the sand and pretend not to know systemic racism has eroded the foundation of humanity? The infamous eight minutes enabled brothers and sisters, regardless of socioeconomic standing, to march arm in arm and demand liberty and justice for all. I challenge you to take 480 seconds out of your day and meditate on how you can be part of the solution.

T R A C I E   M c C A S L I N

Wooden Shoes

Little did I know my first experience of Tulip Time, the third largest tourist attraction, would leave an echo of fear, shame, and embarrassment for more than ten years—all because of stupid wooden shoes. From the time of kindergarten all the way through high school, every child who lived in Holland, Michigan, was required to participate in this festival; it was actually part of our school curriculum. We had to dress in layers like Dutch kids with wooden shoes and march in a parade. Whoever invented wooden shoes has never worn them, it's a blister fest experience. While marching, everywhere you looked was hundreds of thousands of tulips, streets packed with people, bleachers overcrowded and street vendors everywhere. It was hot and extremely uncomfortable wearing layers and layers of clothes and the wooden shoes. You could smell hot dogs, popcorn, cotton candy and my favorite elephant ears. Our cue to begin marching was a high school band playing "Tiptoe Through the Tulips." My stomach doing flips from nervousness. We'd march just a little bit. When the band in front would stop to play, we'd link hands in a circle and dance for the crowd. Dancing in a clockwise position, kicking our feet over our head while wearing the ridiculous wooden shoes. Unfortunately, I ended up kicking my shoe into the crowd, tripping on my skirt and falling on my face. Even broke my nose. More than anything, I was embarrassed. After that experience which was my first, every year I would be a scared nervous wreck when it came time for Tulip Time. I did manage to get through it two more times without broken bones, just lots of blisters from the stupid shoes. To this day, I absolutely still hate everything about Tulip Time except the elephant ears. My son got to experience Tulip Time and loves it, but he has never had to actually participate in it.

Don't Be Cruel

When your day is long, the night seems to grow larger and ever more the quieter. I lay at night, hearing the kids next door play, and my nightmare is made real. My house is empty, my heart aches. The very next door also laughed at me on my way out to the store. One hour later I came in, too many bags in hand, then came a quiet voice. "Excuse me, ma'am, do you need help?" I couldn't speak. This little girl stood there, no older than ten years old. Wavy Brown hair, tennis shoes, and a very big shirt. That little girl looked like someone must love her, she said "No trouble, ma'am, I got you. Lead the way." She helped me in. My music still played low, Elvis Presley's "Don't be Cruel." Her little eyes lit up like the Christmas tree lights.

I couldn't help myself. I asked, "Would you like a drink and snack?" She said, "My mom said I can't take things from people. I shouldn't even be in your house. You seem, like a nice lady so I'll tell you what...if you eat, I'll eat." I laughed at that little girl. She asked, "Where are your kids?" I said, "I don't have any." We danced to Elvis Presley, then she was gone.

Five hours later came a knock on the door. A four-foot-eleven-inch woman stood there with a child behind her. I left the door open and said, "Come in." I allowed this woman to look around. We talked for some hours, we cried and laughed. I shared the fact that I had lost my husband due to the fact I couldn't have kids. He was a cheater, and I was half a woman to him. She had lost her husband to cancer one year before we met. I told her any time she needed, my door was open to her and the kids.

My walls didn't mock me that night. I slept. And two kids were standing at my car the next day. That summer, at least four days a week, I had two little girls at my door—we danced and watched movies. I can't say what I gave them kids, but I know what they left. On one of our last days together, this little lady said, "My mom said you're God sent. There isn't anything cruel about you."

It could take a whole village to bring up a child, yet it takes only one child to fix every hole in anyone's heart.

Open your eyes. What you can't have, will find you, and some things just hurt, and other things just save. How many views do you allow yourself? Me? I learned my best lesson through little eyes.

Roses

It's the one place throughout my childhood where I felt safe and secure. A place where I could be everything I wanted to be. A gold medal gymnast, a secret agent, a bride who would marry her prince underneath the big oak tree, next to the beautiful rose bushes my grandmother cherished.

I was a little girl living inside a universe I created for myself. It was my escape because the real world was harsh and often cruel. I adored my grandmother. She was different than my mother and we had a very special bond.

Those roses were symbolic of that bond: colorful, delicate, spectacular in full bloom.

The day my grandmother passed, they opened in full bloom. A tribute to her—at least that's how I felt—that warm sunny afternoon in May when I said goodbye for now . . .

CAROLYNN PADILLA

Chipped Away

I stood on one side of the old, rickety bridge, looking from one end to the other. I had a light-hearted feeling in my chest as I breathed deeply, inhaling the wet smell from the aging wood that held the bridge together. Somehow this bridge, maybe 50 yards in length, had weathered many storms. Thunderstorms, lightning strikes, snow and blizzards and rainfalls. The sun was showing its joyous face to the west and I couldn't help but smile. A sign from above or merely an every day, natural occurance of nature?

I thought about this for a moment. I guess I have always taken the sunrise for granted, not giving her the credit due. How wonderful she is to see her in her glory, brightening every minute of every day, warming even the coldest of days, browning my pale skin into a golden kiss. And in this moment I feel awakened. A light bulb moment perhaps, and the smile on my face widens.

I feel emotionally alive. For the first time in a long time, I feel hopeful. I have faith in this day and that is all that matters at this moment.

I start to walk across the old, beaten bridge, each step slow and deliberate, a touch of fear quickly fades when I give myself some encouraging self talk. The bridge had been through some beatings, yet still stood tall and proud, surely it wouldn't crumble on my short walk!

I noticed that the paint was chipping off of the railing of the old bridge, a beautiful, cherry colored wood underneath. How radiant the color was, and to think no one would ever see how truly magnificent this old bridge really was unless the paint chipped off of it!

I started to compare myself to the structure, and thought over briefly, all of the storms I had weathered, all the repairs and patches I applied to the outer layers of my soul, a temporary fix . . .

I vowed right there, as I crossed over the old, beautifully worn bridge, that I would shed the outer layers that needed to be chipped away. And once I allowed this process to fully take shape, I would shine from within, with a brand new surface, just as I witnessed as I walked over the bridge to the other side.

What I learned that day, would stay with me forever. How blind we can be to the powerful, strong, beautiful makings of an individual. We look at surfaces. Skimming briefly, what is obviously failing to take the time to go deeper and really appreciate the unique, customized make-ups of who we are.

It may not be pretty to shed the outer layers, letting everything that isn't meant to be there, fall away. But over time, the process takes over and what is meant to transpire, does so, and what is meant to evolve—develops! I am not afraid. I am exhilarated and eager to allow the process to begin.

The rain starts to fall, the clouds cover the sun. I smile, walk slower and enjoy the wetness on my face. For the first time ever, I welcome the downpour and look forward to the rainbow that waits to shine through, after the storm.

Without Shame

I was the happiest person and proudest big sister in the world when you were born, and for 35 years, you have been one of the most important people in my life. I will never understand what life has been like for you, but I am just grateful that more and more in life it has become more acceptable to be gay. Not that it would ever have changed how dad felt about it. I did my very best to try to toughen you up so you wouldn't get abused by our opinionated, hateful father. And I hope you know that though I tried to protect you, I would never want to change you for the world. And you should know that now that I look back, I psychologically acted like a tomboy so he wouldn't want to touch me the way he did . . .

I wanted to be a boy as a self-protection measure, and I was rough with you so he wouldn't say and do things to make you cry and have low self-esteem. I wish I could have been your mom instead of your sister. Things would have been very different. It would have been ok for you to be exactly who you are without shame, just love. I wish I wasn't so broken and could have been a better role model and shown you a better life and been stronger, but all I can do is display that behavior now. I just want you to know that I love you so very much, and I am proud of you and how you have turned your life around, and who you have become in spite of your obstacles. I miss our laughter and playfulness. You're the best brother in the world.

DAWN RICHBURG

My Dedication To You

In 2012, I remember being at my mom's house for a BBQ for my nephew's birthday. I wore white capris with a black girlie tank top with glitter and gold on the shirt. I had a Baby Phat zip-up hoodie that was white and see-through and I had my black and white Jordans on. My dad was doing some work on his Chevy truck so he called me over there to show me. His driver door was open and he was playing the radio and on came a song "Because I Got High" by Afroman. My dad told me, "This is my dedication to you," and I started laughing.

I still remember all the different smells of the BBQ, the kids running around yelling and screaming, everyone drinking and of course the smell of weed in the air. I can still feel the ripples of his seats in the truck, the colors were dark blue, grey, black and white stripes. It was a '72 Chevy block truck, and he had just put a cue ball as his shifter. I can still see the Virgin Mary that he has hanging from the rear view mirror. My dad was funny because he always thought no matter what he did that he was super cool. Anytime I was there and he heard that song he'd turn it up all loud and call for me as he would sing the chorus with the song. It became a thing and now that he's gone, everytime I hear that song from Afroman I think of him.

REBECCA ROMERO

Black Love

Black Love

Brown, caramel, chocolate, to the lightest brown, to the darkest shade of black. Black Love.

When it's truly Black Love, the beauty transcends you. The passion unmatched, the erotica of two Black bodies, bare, thriving, sweaty, trembling together. A Black woman's body, a Black woman's soul, many try to buy it, try to replicate it—the curves, the voluptuous vibrance. But it's something you can only be born with. A real man knows when it's real. The elegance of a Black queen, our hair, our crown, I wear it proud.

Where is my Black Love?

Black Cry

It started off slow, a warm single tear down one incredible Black girl's cheek. Then I cried from my black spirit, I cried from my black skin, with snot and sweat, with a deep howl from the pit of my black belly. I cried from the ghost of my ancestors and the bonds they died with. I cried from my prison cell, from my black sentence. The gigantic streams now flowing as incalculable as the bullets hitting black bodies to the pavements of America's cold black streets. I cried for every

Black man or woman sitting in a cell that could no longer be a parent to lost Black children. I cried from my afro, from my crown. I cried for the images of black bodies hanging lifeless, embedded in my mind. A cry so intense and so sickening and so bottomless to ever heal. A wound birthed to me, to us.

I cried a Black cry . . .

Black Smile

His smile gives me hope. His Black smile makes me warm. His Black smile relieves my soul.

I've never tasted his Black smile or his seemingly soft, chocolate Black lips . . .

Is he my Black love?

Or will he make me Black cry?

For now all I know is

I'm wearing my

Black Smile . . .

Kaleidoscope

To be alone in your own mind. Separate from your true reality, hoping not to breathe, asking not to feel.

Everything lost its value: love, life and mortals. Syringe in my hand watching life in the review. Pushing back all the memories of who I used to be.

Death seemed the only door, worth opening. The only journey towards a future.

My only sensation of peace.

It is like an extra finger. Scraping at the back of my mind pressing, clawing, relinquishing any control I had left in me.

Selling me elusive perceptions of who I ought to be. Numbing out any memory of my fairytale family.

This fever overtook me, weakening, enslaving, stripping, squeezing my soul of all humanity. These drugs chased me right out of reality. While I sit and comprehend why I have been forsaken.

I begin to beseech my reckoning, yearning to belong and love again.

Seeing things through a different lens. Realizing through the kaleidoscope:

"That love is knowing, I am everything.

Wisdom is knowing, I am nothing.

And between the two my life begins."

Mr. Piggy

I'm sorry for letting him tear you apart. You were a cute stuffed piggy. So pretty and pink with a heart that said, "I Love You." You were given to me with a red rose. This was the day he asked me to move in with him. He said, "Anytime I'm not around and you feel sad, alone or afraid, hold on to Mr. Piggy and remember this is a symbol of our love...as long as he is with you I am also there. Remember I will forever love you, Mr. Piggy is witness to our love." When I first held you I was so excited and cried, you made our love real, you were the symbol of this. When we fought I always would hang on to you because, to me, it was a way of clinching onto our love. I wanted him to see you and remember and feel that love he said he felt for me. I wanted you to remind him of our love just as you reminded me of it every time I would hold you. It was also like as long as I could hold you, our love can never fall apart. For some reason how much time passed every time I held you, you always seemed to smell of him. You helped me calm down and go to bed after a long fight where he blamed me for everything and anything. You witnessed every hair pull, every hit. You witnessed our love fall apart! After every fight, you were my comfort. He knew how much you meant to me, to our love. He did anything possible to hurt me, not just physically but what he enjoyed the most were the emotional wounds so deep that to this day, years later, those wounds are still not completely healed. The day he tore you apart, it hurt me so deep I remember running out of air. It was as if, with you tearing apart, our love has been torn with you. There was no repairing the damage. The love was *gone*!

AMBERLEE THEODORATOS

Like the Whisper of a Ghost

My Mother loves me. My mother is one of the most amazing women I know. She always has been, always. That is until the meth addiction took over and left a shell of the woman I once knew. Like the whisper of a ghost. Although rarely, I could still see some of her qualities. She has always felt like home. Even now as a shell. Which may be the very reason that I could stay. It's like a train wreck, everyone wants to look, and no one knows how to stop and help.

When I was younger, she was my best friend. That may be part of the problem too. I wanted to go where she went, do what she did, see what she saw. I've outpassed her now and seen and done far too much. For so long, I had seen an obscured view of safety. Who could possibly be safer than mom? She was always so much fun. She is so beautiful, so kind and patient and understanding. She glows. Well, she did. Now I rarely see a glimmer in her eyes.

Where has she gone? People flock to her, they love to be around her. She is so giving. Too giving. They take advantage. Maybe when they took advantage, they also took some of the glimmer? She felt so much at one time. So much compassion for the human race. A smile from a stranger would highlight her week. The smallest mishaps made her feel so guilty. So human. That may be part of the problem.

Her guilt at times is too much for her to handle. She has now found a way to numb it out. She's so loyal, sometimes too loyal. I think I picked that up from her . . . that, and my toes. Especially the middle ones.

She will never stop feeling like home. She is worth saving, but I can't save her, not when I know I am safe.

Sometimes I wonder if this is what it feels like to be a parent? If this is what it feels like to lose a child to drugs. That clear existence, so transparent, but so full of her soul.

Limon Correctional Facility

HERBERT ALEXANDER

Real Pain

A late-night phone call is how B. received the news of his brother's tragic death. Unprepared mentally to absorb the information, his acumen led him to believe that he was stuck in a nightmare. But he wasn't, not even close; the shit just got real. Without receiving any details of the critical juncture, he knew in his heart his brother T's death was a result of gun play. An assumption that was soon to be proven correct. T., at 19, was shot in the heart with a .357 and died alone in the middle of the street. Without any family or true friends, just him and the unforgiving night. B. could only think of how scared he must've been, by himself, lying on that cold pavement. How much pain he felt as he struggled to reach for his last breath. How his mother will handle the impact of losing her youngest son. How his sister will function after losing the brother she was closest to. How does a man deal with that type of pain, all while trying to balance the scales of revenge and guilt? Retaliation was inevitable, life in a box was inevitable, until the inevitable look from the eyes of B.'s wife and child, halted all negative possibilities.

*

Years later I held my wife for the last time as a free man, and in that moment, nothing else seemed to matter. It was as if the world stopped and the weight of my sins no longer existed. Nevertheless, it didn't take long before reality dealt its crushing blow. The courts were merciless, sentencing me to an eye-popping 64 years. *What the fuck?* was my only expression to the judge. As I watched my life dissolve through the lens of salty tears, emotionless, all I felt was an embarrassing sense of stupidity. Damn! I just left my beautiful wife alone to raise our two boys. My relationship is over, she'll never forgive me for this one. But years later she did. Stating that her love is unconditional and she wouldn't leave me alone to rot, and once more, it felt as if nothing else seemed to matter.

Then, without warning, life hit me with another ton of bricks. My wife had to be hospitalized for days due to an extreme seizure caused by lupus. A feeling of terror engulfed my body with every thought of potentially losing her. Although she was the one suffering, I can honestly say, I experienced real pain. Sitting in a cell, pleading with God, to please guarantee her recovery, so I can have the chance to be a better husband and one day pay back all the love she had given me, because I just can't afford to have someone else I love die alone.

DEXTER LEWIS

The Man in the Mirror

It had gone too far, he should've never crossed the narrow threshold that defined the terms and conditions of his release. He just couldn't help feeling closed in, confined to a room not much bigger than his old prison cell. Sounds from the nightlife vandalized his wild imagination. Reaching the point of no return, one dubious step followed another and the hunt was on. The who, what, when, where and how was yet to be determined. This was all part of his thrill-seeking nature.

Curiosity consumed him. Now it seemed as if he'd been held back in the same grade. Failing yet again, back in the same predicament that changed everything in the first place. It was the crazy cycle spinning out of control, but this time was different. This time he would have to make a crucial decision. It was simple, "turn back or die."

*

I wish I would've taken heed to them saying, "if you continue down that road, you'll never..." It was too late. My mind was fixed, and besides, who can save a man on the run determined to go nowhere fast? So, I ran and ran, faster and further. A desperate soul, eager to find a life worth living. Eager to make leaps and bounds from a past "for-giving," "for-getting," I wanted nothing to do with.

Off in the distance I see an old timer standing in the middle of a dirt road. He casually waves me over. This obviously was no ordinary man. We stood about the same height, his features eerily akin to my own. He wore a dusty robe worn to rags with an empty look on his face. Hatred trapped poison within the territories of his mind. He was crippled by the haunting facts of a troubled past, serving as a constant reminder of sure damnation.

"Ol' youngster," he said in a soft yet confident tone. "I was just like you once, long ago. You would probably never guess, I've been around for millennia. Seen it all, done it all, that's a fact. These are the last days before the great Armageddon of the Gemini. Everyone's afraid to die, but the truth is...no one knows if the grass is greener on the other side. If you continue down this road, through the screens and the smoke, you'll arrive in the city of the vultures. It beamed with life before the purge of the savages. Now blood and bones clone a dead-ridden culture." As I listened to the cries of this crazed man, I realized that I was standing in a broken mirror. I shook my head in disbelief, but couldn't hide the shame. I couldn't recognize the reflection staring back, it was unfamiliar.

I was off again before he got another word in. Determined to get somewhere. Anywhere, but back there. The world emerged into nothing more than a muddled memory. On the surface, I was sprinting, but inside, my humanity was slipping away. Just ahead, another figure appeared, dwelling directly in my pathway. As I drew near, the crazed man I left in the dust a ways back had reemerged. This was either a strange case of déjà vu or I was definitely hallucinating. He was bolting in my direction. His eyes like wicks illuminating a depraved vessel. It was fight or flight for me, and of course, I did what I do best. "Run, run, run..." every bone in my body screamed. I turned swiftly, crashing hard and fast. We locked eyes as I tumbled clumsily to the ground. "Just like you, just like you..." he repeated like a broken record stuck on the same loop. The fire in his eyes revealed a man dancing in eternal flames, wallowing in sin. Just then it dawned on me, I'd been the one broken, standing in the mirror, facing my demons. There was nowhere to run. All along I was trying to get away, but never stopped to realize that it was my thoughts holding me captive all the while. The mental chains bound me to the boundaries of self-doubt and I had the key to release them. So, I faced the man in the mirror today. He was a scared, beaten, and broken boy dressed in grown-up skin. I had to lay the child to rest in silent slumber. Today, a boy became a man.

Europa

Of the countless songs that remind me of my teenage years, none transport me back to that extraordinary time like Santana's breathtaking classic, "Europa." The guitar launches into an enchanting opening phrase, and in a flash, I'm 17 again, standing inches from the entrance of a stage in an old dusty schoolyard in northeast Denver. I can hardly breathe. Or stand. The weight of the guitar strapped to my body nearly crushing the life out of me. Overhead, high above the city lights, stars shimmer against the velvet sky like pieces of shattered glass. "It's do or die," I say to myself, hoping to rally whatever strength I have in me. But before the words can leave my lips, an eruption of applause fills the space around me. The lights go dark as a group of actors exit the stage. A crude concoction of fear and excitement suddenly hijacks my body. My heart—now in my throat—races uncontrollably, and my legs feel like they are made of Jell-O. I'm teetering on the precipice of an abyss, staring deeply into the unknown, feeling more alive than ever, moments away from getting my first taste of what it's like to perform in front of an audience.

After weeks of anticipation and rigorous rehearsals, my time to shine had finally arrived. It was El Centro Su Teatro's third annual summer showcase, which at the time—1989—was located at the old Elyria elementary school. I spent my summer there learning about theater and music and hangin' with other artists. It was there that I discovered, for the first time, what it was like to experience a sense of community, to share space with a group of people who are very much like me. And there I was, waiting for my cue, feeling every passing second as if each was an eternity.

I spent all summer learning to play that damn song! Hour after hour. Playing the tape, picking out the notes on my guitar one at a time, and rewinding and playing it back again and again. I wore the hell outta that stupid tape. But, in the end, all my hard work paid off. I got it! Hell, yeah, I got it. And I was ready to play it for the world. "Ladies and gentlemen . . . " announced the emcee, " . . . make some noise for Mr. Joaquin Mares." After a generous round of applause, followed by a moment of deafening silence, my cousin/rhythm guitarist signaled me with a nod. Then, a sudden surge of energy shot through me as my fingers boldly ripped into the opening phrase to "Europa."

Many years have passed since then, but I remember that moment like it was yesterday. Not only because it was my first public performance, but more importantly, because of the people I shared that experience with. It was an absolute honor and privilege to have had such a momentous opportunity. Su Teatro is truly the reason I relive that moment whenever I hear the song "Europa."

ADRIAN MARTINEZ

Sitting Here

Sitting in this cell with my mind everywhere but here. My thoughts meander around until these cracked and peeling walls of isolation fade, leaving me to be defined by the physical embodiment of the words that confine with their very purpose.

I pace this concrete floor which feels eternal as I sift my past, present and future. I am desperate in my helplessness to find where I went wrong.

Love, honor, guilt, loyalty, faithfulness and betrayal, all to be examined with a delicate touch . . .

Rare is the time I do this right, so again, they hit me like a flood threatening to pull me under and away from the reality that is me.

My mind is strong, yet doubt clouds me with the physical touch. I stumble in mid stride. I steady myself on the stainless-steel basin, catching a glimpse of the man in the mirror, the look we exchange in that brief instant expresses the need to arm myself. So, I reach out to the piece of me, that has never failed or given way, always keeping me warm and safe. I surrender my mind and soul to the very essence of hate.

Yet to hold it is to feel the burns of the fires of the past. Fear holds me not. For now, hate is my slave, I can hold it and mold it to my will, devastating those around me with no thought or care of the pain that will follow from being such a callous master.

I was forged in the inferno that is hate, so care matters not when you are being tempered by such an emotion.

Time slows down and stops . . . I look around and embrace the destruction that holds me in its grip, giving me comfort and safety from the love and peace that searches for me.

For the sister of love is trust and the enemy of trust is never far behind: betrayal. "Only those who you trust can betray you," a lesson I hold close in the solitude of mine. Love leaves you with the physical definition of the word, alone, while betrayal leaves you with an emptiness that defines you as a void ever after.

Insolent, I laugh as the fires of the past burn my most deepest memories. My name is hollow and I hide in the emptiness that is me.

Barely escaping the tears I know would drown me if given release. I sit in the corner of this concrete cage, free from all feeling, blind by rage . . . I breathe . . . I collect myself . . . With my head down I catch a peek out of the corner of my eye, I see what holds and protects me from the lashes of my hate. It stands and waits by the rusting metal door of my imprisonment, offering me solace in a doorway of a different kind . . . Shall I relinquish my fight or just allow it to be?

I'm just sitting here.

Love, Compassion and Madness

This matriarch was the most beautiful mixture of love, compassion and madness. Looking at her then, all I could see was the madness. The chicken she sat in front of me smelled delicious, she had put her heart into cooking this meal. The heat from the chicken warmed my skin. Not wanting to be burned, I sat silently with anticipation while the chicken cooled. She looked at me with the most beautiful smile on her face and went back to eating.

Her smile reminded me of the time she taught me how to fish. I was running towards her. In my right hand, I held my fishing pole, (my brand new ugly stick), and in my left, I held a cup of worms. With a little too much zeal to reach her, I tripped and fell, dropping everything. She came over and helped me to my feet, she smiled and said, "Everyone falls, it's the getting back up that's important."

However, sitting at the supper table I found myself embraced by relief, because prior, similar situations were not met with a smile. I decided to sit there a few more moments. I knew when I made that decision I was playing Russian roulette with a fully-loaded gun. She looked at me again. The love and compassion had escaped her. My heart started to beat faster and my throat was so dry I couldn't have swallowed a bite if I was forced to. "Why aren't you eating?" she asked. "It's too hot," I replied. She looked at me, the fire in her eyes grew hotter than the chicken. I waited for words, but all I got was action. She jumped up from the table and with three very calculated movements, she reached over my mother's plate to mine, grabbed the chicken off my plate, threw it in the freezer and slammed the door. "That ought to cool that shit off for you," she said. That was one of many memories I have of my grandma, the matriarch of our broken family.

My grandma always spoke using idioms. The one she used the most was after we said somethins she didn't like or thought was stupid. She would say, "That sounds like Greek to me!" It was often a challenge piecing together meaning out of her secret way of speaking. Being a homemaker to a husbandless and childless home, my grandma sought comfort in cooking and botany. My grandma lit up most when her shows came on, *Young and the Restless, One Life to Live*, and so on. I'm still not sure how she kept up with all of them. I'd come over to visit and she would tell me all about her shameless indulging. At first it bored me to no end. As time went on, I began to really enjoy her version of the shows she watched, so much so that, when I grew up, I enjoyed the same shows myself. At times, my grandma and I were poles apart; at other times, we were cast in the same mold. One day my grandma grabbed my hand and sat me down. She looked me in the eyes and said, "The world's not a nice place." That was the end of our conversation. I've lived every day learning that lesson. My eyes have never seen a different grandma. She was always the same with everyone she met, she was always on schedule and she showed love, compassion and madness to everyone she met. I've learned to do the same.

Blue Boys Bicycle

I've been bought, sold, stolen and bartered more times than I care to count. I've spent countless hours, days, weeks, months and even years idly waiting for someone to take me out. I know naught of sadness, so the waiting doesn't affect my spirit. Only my age and its consequences. My paint is oxidized, my seat is cracked. But my mechanics are still intact and ready to roll in a moment's notice.

Not much to look at, I know. But still totally functional and with a little oil and new rubber, I'd be reliable for thousands more miles. And with a complete makeover, some paint and polish, I could one day become a sought-after collectible.

In the beginning, I was given as a birthday present to little Bobby. It took him a while to get his balance but before long, we rode all over the countryside. Up hills, down hills, over small jumps. "Wee He He He He He!" His energy was infectious. So much so that even an inanimate object like a blue boy's bicycle inherited his spirit and enthusiasm. "Wee He He He He He!" He would yell at the top of his lungs as he peddled with all his might, and we would slice through the air like a jet plane. We were partners, Bobby and me. And few were the days that we didn't spend time together going someplace. Or no place at all. It was enough that we had the freedom to just go.

Oh, we had our crashes. Skinned elbows and knees, and more than a few flat tires. But never did we consider slowing down. It was just in either of us to not want to cut through the air and make our own wind as fast as we could go. "Wee He He He He He!"

But boys grow up to be men and Bobby moved on to new and exciting ventures. It's been years now. And I'm still eager to go. Still as reliable as your legs are able to peddle. And still longing for the excitement and joy of a happy young pilot yelling "Wee He He He He He!" as we peddle off into the horizon.

Sterling Correctional Facility

Corndog

Remember when your wife was unfaithful? It was awful when and how you found out, right? You could clearly recall the phone call from your lovely mother-in-law all while you were driving around in the corndog. The corndog? An old and ugly brown Toyota pickup. The kids called it the corndog, and you thought it was a cute name because *they* named it.

You pulled in front of your in-laws place, knowing that your wife was inside. She had something to tell you she said, so you arrived quickly. She had moved out of the house right before you were both evicted. Coward, you probably thought. She was staying with her mother for a while, "to figure some things out," she explained.

Stepping inside with no hellos, you found your wife in one of the spare bedrooms crying. The sorrow felt was thick and greasy, it clung to every surface. Sitting on the bed next to your wife, you listened as she willingly confessed all of the selfish things that she had been doing secretly. Secretly with someone else.

Devastation cannot even begin to describe your hurt. Falling on the floor you began to weep, yell, swear. That got you nowhere, but it felt oddly satisfying. All she and her mother could do was nod. The power was yours. The pain was wrenching. You obviously had to make a tough choice, right there and right then.

Whatever *could* be done would not be easy. Would it be worth it, whatever it was? Even though your pain was dreadful, witnessing her personal agony broke you. Yet your heart was able to speak to you.

Softly, it had whispered to you what to say, what to do. You had your own choice, and then she had one too. You asked her to stay there with her mother. You asked her to get in the corndog and came home.

Somehow, over some time, things would get better. You were thinking that while quietly driving home. Those precious seeds of forgiveness were being sown as your wife sat in the seat next to you.

CRAIG FORBES

The Smile of a Painter

An empty wall? Cold desolate concrete, alone and isolated, empty and in mourning. Going about every day without meaning, its only task is to confine. Is this what the wall aspires to be? Was this the hope of its creator? Does the concrete shed tears for its lack of purpose? Does it yearn for more? I can feel the porous grey expanse, calling out to me, begging me to expose its inner beauty, to deliver it from its life of confining. It pleads for a purpose to hide its emptiness. It dreams of being saturated in strokes of color; I *will* deliver it unto beauty for in doing so I will deliver myself.

Empty arms, not hollow, only featureless. Forced into a life that isn't their own. Living an existence of survival, no dreams, only the nightmares of reality. They feel an inner worth yet must fight for survival. To masquerade, as the marauders, if only for comfort and security. No longer empty, after many years of the journey, adorned and marked, images of death, dark and menacing, just to fade into the perceived reality.

Hollow eyes, lost and confused, confused from a world that strives to close them forever. Hiding their pain, choking back their tears. Yearning for brighter days, but afraid to remove the shades, so many years spent in darkness makes the light an uncomfortable sight. In the mirror lost to what or who I actually see. Is this me? Is this me. So many layers of face, so complex, so many scars. Who am I? Who has it been chosen for me to be?

A life of black and grey, now bathed in color, relishing its radiance and beauty. I am a simple painter, a meaningless term for many, but oh so extravagant of an existence for me. I bring meaning and light to the cold concrete walls both inside and outside of my heart. My face now masquerades under a smile. no longer living a lie, or am I ?

I want to be happy, I want to love, I want to laugh, but at times I feel like I have forgotten how. I guess the only expression I am capable of is at the tip of my paintbrush.

JESSE LYNCH

Diluted Sunshine

As the only room in the basement with a window you would think people would have been fighting to claim it as their own. For all of the crampedness of the space, it still has a bit of diluted sunshine which reached its walls everyday. It began happy enough—freshly painted, new carpet laid, ready to receive its boarders. Maybe as a nursery, possibly a toy room, the potential for it to bring joy was unlimited. As the neighborhood transformed around it, so did the room. The nice children no longer lived there. Instead of the gentle sound of a child dreaming or the joyous laughter of new toys being discovered there was yelling, fighting and blaring electronics.

All of the love once held within the room became hate and misery. The room tried to maintain its dignity; stoically holding its position while holes were punched into its door, never wincing when its carpet was melted into a tough green polyester crust, not making a sound when the walls were scratched and soiled. It tried to love the families that came after its first love, the family who really loved it back. The best family that kept its walls painted, its carpet clean and its windows washed.

This new family was different, they did not care about how it looked or felt. They seemed to revel in the torture. The first time the pipe in the closet burst, the room was filled with water and shame. When the new people let it fester for days, the water and shame became disgust. Its ruined carpet was a soppy and swollen reminder of the neglect. The fire was almost a relief, a chance to be reborn through smoke and fire.

Instead of rebirth, there was only ugly scars crusted into the carpet, and the boy who always cried.

There was sadness for the boy, yet he was the one who set the fire; he brought destruction upon the room too. The boy deserved sympathy, yet the room has none left to give. The love was gone! Washed away by water and smoke, neglect and purposeful destruction. It began to rebel. To creak and moan its displeasure day and night. It cracked its own windows, once its pride and joy, now only a tool for its anger. Let the elements in! Wind! Water! Dust! Creatures! Critters! All are welcome to witness revenge.

What was once a cradle is now a coffin. The filth sunk deep within its spirit, the first love song forgotten, the dark and damp now its accomplice. Wishing for its own destruction it finds solace in the terror it wreaks and feels. It imagines itself as splinters returning to the dirt from which it came. And then all was quiet. For once, the people were quiet. They moved like ghosts. Filling bags and boxes. They exchanged rushed whispers as they delicately closed doors. They didn't return the next day. Or the next. Or the next. They were gone. Scattered toys, books and clothes remained behind. I wonder what the next people will be like? Will they fix the scars? Will they understand the gnashing and groaning?

DOUGLAS MICCO

Reckless Abandon

Growing up in small-town Kansas was wonderful. We had easy access to both city and country living. My family lived on the edge of town surrounded by farm pasture. There were ponds, creeks and the woods. There was also a big river on the north end of town.

The summers were clear and free! From the moment the school doors burst open we were on vacation! I spent all of my time outdoors running and playing in the fields and barns. I also rode my bicycle around our neighborhood. Of course I was never satisfied with both wheels on the ground. I wanted to jump over school busses, livestock, and the clouds. All of this courtesy of my little plywood ramp laying on a few bricks.

We rode ponies, horses and cattle. I learned quickly that milk-cows do not appreciate anyone trying to ride them, to include a 70-pound nine year old. I hopped on ponies and horses without a second thought, bridle, or saddle and tore out into the fields. I would get thrown off horses, fall off or crash in the bushes. One time I got clotheslined by a cottonwood tree limb as I went galloping into the timber. After a while, we wore our steeds down to submission and they followed our commands. I learned how to make my horse jump over fences, bound through ponds, and I took to riding on their backs while standing up. We rode with reckless abandon. I was oblivious to danger, and pain could be rubbed off with few tears shed. I spilled blood on sunflowers and tore skin on barbed wire as a meadowlark trilled in laughter.

Baseball was a mad passion and we played with vigor. If you didn't know how to play, we would teach you. We used dry cow patties for the bases and a piece of metal served as home plate. Before we yelled "Play ball!" we commenced to arguing and quarreling over the rules of the field since we had five bases instead of the customary four bases, altering our baseball diamond into a pentagon. We yelled and screamed as we played, as if our national security depended upon it.

Running and playing in the woods under the big, blue Kansas sky, we lept from one fallen tree to the next. We dared each other to jump from cliffs over creeks and streams, sometimes climbing trees, vaulting limb to limb. We tossed big rocks to see who could make the biggest splash. We searched the water for fish, polliwogs and snakes. We romped through the river bottom and played under the canopy of timber, into our imaginations and to other worlds.

My army declared war on great beasts and attacked with fervor. Sticks turned to spears, dirt clods became grenades which exploded on impact and rocks were projectile missiles. We led the onslaught until it was time to go home for supper.

We walked away victorious having conquered this wicked creature. Our defeat over this old mossy fallen tree.

TIMOTHY NICHOLLS

I Can Only Imagine

For centuries music has impacted the human condition like few things. Music has always been a passion of mine, even from childhood when I learned to read music and play the saxophone. I've enjoyed numerous genres, but nothing has moved me as deeply as worship music. From Southern gospels to hymns, contemporary to exquisite instrumentals, worship songs stir my spirit, drawing me ever closer to my creator.

Not many months after 9/11, I experienced my own personal tragedy, losing three loved ones in one night, which devastated my world. I had lost everything, with pain and hopelessness my new companions. The grief was unbearable, yet music occasionally provided solace and healing, revising my spirit for a short while. For months I searched for some relief from the anguish through music, hoping to soothe the rage within.

Far too often, music would awaken and evoke these memories, wonderful moments of dancing to our favorite songs, watching those beautiful smiles stretch across angelic faces as they sang along, twirling like little ballerinas or posing as rock stars. Part of me just wanted it all to end, and music began to drive me to the brink of madness. But when I heard worship music everything was much, much different,

One autumn evening, the crisp air rolling in through an open window, I drove around seeking rest, finding none. As the aspens turned their golden brown and with a hint of rain in the air, I wandered aimlessly, with my digital jukebox spewing out rock, country, jazz, R & B, and everything in between, I sought peace, but found none. But something deep within me stirred and led me to the lower end of the

FM band, but why?

All that was to me was talk radio and sports. But I searched it anyway. Then I heard it. A piano, lonely notes ringing out in my truck, my brain began to stir, I paused. Basic structure, simple notes caught my ear. I drove, not knowing my destination, but I searched, with a prayer of finding one. Then I heard the words "I can only imagine, " which flowed through the speakers and into my soul.

"Surrounded by your glory, what will my heart feell . . . " I hadn't felt anything good in months, now a wellspring of emotion surged across the expanse of my being. I had sought comfort in the Lord before but I felt so distant from Him. As the song continued to play, I pulled into an empty lot to let this song, and my God, embrace me. "Will I stand in your presence, or to my knees will I fall . . ." Tears flowed, and for the first time I knew I wasn't alone.

A kaleidoscope of joyful memories and blessings played on the IMAX of my mind, pictures of love and devotion, playfulness and glee, good times and bad. "Will I sing Hallelujah? Will I be able to speak at all? I can only imagine . . ." As the words saturated my core, my mind seemed to cascade into nothingness, trapped by this senseless loss, yet there's something more.

Darkness everywhere. A trillion light years from the life I had, now lost in the void. But the Lord once said, "Let there be light." And there was...faint, distant. So far away, untouchable. Moments stretch into hours as the bridge repeats, "I can only imagine." I focused on the light. It got brighter, soon I am Mercury to Sol, enveloped so there is no darkness at all. "I can only imagine, when all I would do, is forever, forever worship you, I can only imagine."

As the song faded, the light of His glory subsided, and I was back in reality, the place of loss and hurt. But, something was different. For the first time in months, I hurt a little less. The ache was dull now. It was His gift to me in that moment. Thank you, Father, for such a gentle and beautiful reminder that even though we may experience great sadness, loss or pain, you do wipe away every tear and make way for something much greater: hope. Hope in You.

BRETT PHILLIPS

Impact

Bull in the ring—the maker of men it is called. Much of your life is experienced in these football rituals. Much of life is explained. Boys clad in armor are numbered off. They stand in a circle, arms-length apart, waiting in anticipatory perdition. Anxiety. Fear. Mania. Mouths void of moisture, void of speech, kids eye each other with suspicion and expectation as one steps into the middle. In a sport dictated by forcible impacts, by mass colliding with mass, this one pitiless ritual can make or break you. It made me.

Growing up a boy in Oklahoma in the 1970's, you loved football. It was more than a sport. It was a rite of passage, a way to claim superiority and bragging rights from other towns, other schools, other neighborhoods. As a youngster, my Saturdays were spent in the front yard. My friends and I threw the ball around, practiced jukes, tackles and touchdown poses. In the fall, the University of Oklahoma game was blaring on a boom box. We argued over which player we were. J.C. Watts, George "Buster" Rhymes, Billy Sims. I was always Louie Selmon. We didn't care what the weather was like or anything else for that matter. Football was king.

In the seventh grade, my school had an open tryout to play junior high football. I was always a smallish boy, so the idea of football in pads was daunting. The pressure to play well and to succeed weighed heavily on me. What if I was the next Selmon brother? I would be known, not as some socially awkward, glasses-wearing, smart kid, but as a football star. No more being picked last. No more painful shyness.

No more debilitating uncertainty. I would be somebody.

Coach Miller, a fire-plug of a man, much more agile than his large frame belied, strode around the circle making certain everyone had been numbered. In his quintessential coach's voice, full of authority, doom and drawl, he explained the drill.

"Keep your head on a swivel," he prescribed. "Meet your attacker. Be aware of him and meet him head-on. Find him and attack him."

Under the unrelenting summer sun he walked into the ring, on a dry field by the school building, goat head stickers crunching under his feet. He looked each of us right in the eye, making sure he saw us all. When my gaze met his, I shuddered nervously as I felt the truth of this moment. This was the time: retreat or announce myself to the world. My fear was palpable as the sweat rolled down my face. My cheap Riddell helmet was strapped as tight as I could get it. An ill-fitted mouthpiece pushed my lips apart and my shoulder pads felt like a millstone.

"Men, there's nothing more important than knowing and understanding your surroundings." As he pointed to the circle, he continued, "If he has his back to you, you hit him. We must see what's coming at us; be aware of what's coming. You'll learn to keep your head on a swivel." And then it began.

"Twelve!" Coach Miller barked. CRACK! resounded across the field as a young man hurtled toward the "bull," and was met in beautiful violence. "Four!" BOOM! "Fifteen!" CRASH! "Six!" THUD!

My number was eventually called and immediately I sprinted toward the center. A loud crash echoed through my ears. I realized I had been knocked to my backside. My cheeks reddened with shame as I quickly scrambled to get back to my spot in the ring.

Coach kept asking for volunteers to get in the middle, and my nervousness grew each time I failed to answer the call. Finally, I reached the terminus. I had to either act with courage or shrink in fear. When I stepped into the arena, Coach looked at me dubiously. He asked the right question. "Are you sure you're ready?" he said, lacking malice but instead full of compassion and care. I nodded. I was ready.

What happened next was a blur. I remember all of my repressed feelings of anger, of being ignored, of being less-than coming to the surface in a righteous rage. A holy flame bolstered me from the beating I took. I remember resolving not to give up as wave after wave of much larger opponents bore down on me. Knocking me down. Getting back up. Knocking me down. Getting back up. I remember tears stinging my eyes and mucus mixed with coppery blood running down my face as emotions too intimate to describe poured out of me. And then, it was over.

I heard Coach's voice gently calling to me as my chest heaved with viscous sobs. "What's your name, son?"

He broached the circle as I choked out my own name. He put his meaty hands on my shoulders and with fire in his eyes peered directly into my timid soul. He said something with such kindness, with such love, that it shook my foundation, and changed my life forever. "That . . . is exactly what I'm looking for, that kind of effort. That heart is what it takes to excel in football. Son, don't ever give that up." Head lowered, exhilarated, emotionally exhausted, embarrassed, I left the circle.

There is more to the game of football than offense and defense, wins and losses, tackles and touchdowns. Certainly these things are important parts, but the greater truths, the life lessons are much less obvious. Teamwork, loyalty, self-confidence, work ethic, persistence, overcoming adversity, these are things that the game teaches. But this man, this coach, taught much more than that. What he taught me were much deeper lessons. To me, there are three virtues above all else: faith, hope and love. But the greatest of these is love.

ATORRUS RANIER

A Moment of Trying

When will the beginning of my life start? Having a mother who tries and still not there. But what is your *own* truth? My mother's mother wasn't there either. We're somehow in the moment of trying. At sixteen, what can you do without structure? And now as I am, home so high no closer to finding myself. Sitting on my futon bed feeling heavier than necessary with words bleeding with my heart. With all that's going on with me, do we have a moment for us? My mother walks in my room, a room no bigger than my cell now, with dirty carpet and a T.V. in a corner hoping no one will watch it. And with my mother's presence the walls feel like they're closing in.

This is it! My heart rises between my lips. A tidal wave of truth. No, she's not here about my wrongdoing. She is here about my stolen car parked outside. I parked it wrong, and I need to move it before the cops come. With a hard swallow my heart slides back to hiding. Can I feel more alone than this moment? Can I—we—remember when we ever talked? How do I know you are my mother? Am I the son of the world? It's hard for us, but there is change in us. But time won't let us think beyond ourselves.

As a young adult as you were, I know you see the same pain growing in me, as it did you. Yes, you know my pain, I am you, so I guess we both don't know how to respond with uplifting feedback. I do love you, mother, the only way I know how. And holding onto the gift of unsurety. Somehow and some way seems okay.

Having this woman as my mother showed me that my road will be long and hard. Seeing sunsets and moon rises, never parting, echoing our life as one. Connected but never united.

The Greatest Teacher

My mentor and greatest rock over the years has turned out to be my first real teacher and mentor in my life, my kindergarten teacher Mr. Parker. It's been a strange relationship sometimes; however, it has been long-lasting, honest, loving and very sincere, very father-son like.

The first memory I have of Mr. Parker isn't the best. As a matter of fact, it was very emotionally scary and overwhelming to me. I was only five and jumping right into new beginnings or a new journey was foreign to me. Let me explain what this means to me. I had only recently immigrated from Mexico to the United States, so the English language, school and kindergarten were very scary things to me at five. To make matters worse, Mr. Parker was the first African-American I had ever come across or seen.

Later on in life, Mr. Parker explained to me that his first day of class was always the highlight of his year, getting to know all his kids, the new smells, the new faces, including all of our crazy behaviors. He has had so many experiences with first days of class in his teaching career, but ours stands out to him.

There I was, five years old, kicking, screaming and even clawing at my mama. I begged her not to leave me alone with this man, in a strange land, in some strange place with strange people. But to my amazement and surprise, he spoke Spanish with my mom, reassuring her all would be all right, and that I was in good hands. I don't know how long it took for me to stop crying or to close my mouth and meet my new classmates. Still, to this day, I hear his soft-mannered yet deep, comforting voice speaking Spanish and English to us all.

It's been very difficult for me to adjust to this new country, to a new environment and overall a new world. But over the years, beginning in kindergarten, Mr. Parker has been like a father and mentor to me. He has always checked in on me, tutoring me to help me pick up my grades, trying to make me an overall better person. He's done things for me and my little brother even my own father never did. Unfortunately, I started acting out and rebelling very young, constantly getting into trouble in school and in life. Yet, through it all, Mr. Parker has remained a constant in my life, even to this day.

Mr. Parker will say he is only doing what comes naturally to him. Always the humble and quiet type, he never seeks attention or recognition in all that he contributes to others. He is the greatest example of selflessness and overwhelming generosity.

He has been the sole source of inspiration to me to become better in all that I do. He has given me the greatest example on how to become a better human being. He is very caring, very honest, and very sincere in all that he does. On more occasions than I can count, he has guided me, advised me or mentored me through difficult times in my life. Without Mr. Parker—my teacher, my mentor, the person I call Pops (only because he is older now!)—I would not be the person I am today.

Since very young, I've been in and out of the juvenile system. I've been in the adult system since I was 18. I cannot explain how grateful I am to him and how much more blessed my life has been having him to help guide me through difficult times. It's crazy how that tall, scary, African-American man has become such a source of inspiration and admiration for me. He isn't only my kindergarten teacher or mentor now; he is family to me and the rest of my Mexican familia. Because of people like him, this world is a far better place.

Of course, he would say: "It is nothing" and maybe even suggest I am exaggerating in my praise of him. But that would be Mr. Parker being himself and putting the needs of others ahead of his own. Where he has learned such things and why he chose to bless me and my family, is a mystery to us all. It has been great to choose him and have had him choose me.

Nothing I can say or do will ever show how grateful and fortunate I have been with him here, in my life. I do hope that in sharing such a small sample of our life together with other people, it will help me try. I wish everyone I know could experience and share a friendship like ours. Not only would they be better off for it, but their world would also be much better off. I will forever be indebted and grateful to Mr. Parker—my mentor, my father figure, my kindergarten teacher.

A Lesson from a Stranger

I was just nine years old, sitting on a train in a country I knew little about at that age. Their customs and traditions were totally different than what I knew. I was in Japan because I was a military brat. It was the second place I had moved in two months' time. I hated leaving all my friends behind.

As I sat on that train, it was gray and rainy outside. I was already in a bad mood, surrounded by strangers who I could not talk to. I could not speak their language. They could not speak mine. I'm out of place, just a white kid from Chicago.

Looking around I saw people who were tired and heading home from work. There was no friendly conversation, it seemed like everyone was always looking at the ground. I felt more and more uncomfortable by the minute; not wanting to get caught staring, I focused on the window across the way from where I was sitting. The speed of the train caused the rain drops to streak sideways across the window. The outside world flew by so fast. Along with the dark overcast, it was impossible to recognize anything.

As I sat there, the stop-and-go motion of the train making stops was almost enough to put me to sleep. I turned to the translator assigned to me by my uncle's office.

"How much longer?"

"Not long."

I couldn't get more than two or three words at a time out of this guy. That was so frustrating. I settled back into my seat and resumed once again, my uncomfortable silence and observation of my surroundings.

I tried to make it look like I wasn't watching people, even though that's exactly what I was doing. I realized that everyone was sitting with their hands on laps, palms down, feet flat on the floor. My hands were on the seat, so I wouldn't rock back and forth. I'm so short my feet did not touch the ground. I hated the silence. Broken only by the sound of the train sliding over the tracks, and the thud of the wheels as it hit the next rail. I put my headphones on and turned them up. Music always has a way of calming me down. My mom always said that music is my life. I would always be humming or singing no matter what I was doing. It was my go-to when I was stressed. Me and music were like Linus and his blanket on "Charlie Brown," always together.

I got lost in my music after a few minutes and I started to swing my legs a little. I was feeling good. The stops began to fly by for me . . . lost in my own world. That's when I noticed a scuff on my shoe as I swung my leg.

Now, I'm a shoe guy, a scuff on my shoe will drive me crazy. If I can't get a scuff off my shoe, that's it, I will give them to my brother or to a friend. People knew that and would mess with me by trying to step on my shoes. Sometimes I would change my shoes two or three times in one day. It was so frustrating that a small scuff on my shoes did that to me.

I tried to ignore the scuff on my shoe as I sat on the train. I kept telling myself, "I'll take care of it as soon as I get back to the base." I listened to my music, but as hard as I tried, I could not forget about my scuffed shoe. I told myself, "Just don't cause attention!" I lifted my foot and placed it across my knee. I licked my thumb, to rub the scuff mark.

Before my thumb got close to my shoe, the man next to me reached over...and pushed my foot off my knee. When I looked up at him, he was already facing forward again. I wondered if my translator saw what happened. No luck. His eyes were closed as if asleep, and once again I looked at the man. His eyes were still forward, as if nothing happened.

I sat there for a few moments thinking, was this guy messing with me? Once again, I lifted my foot to try and work on the scuff. Once my foot hit my knee the man pushed it off. When I looked at him this time . . . we made eye contact. He gave me a firm look of disapproval before he faced forward once again. Before he could even settle, I removed my headphones and picked up my foot to place it on my knee. He grabbed my ankle and held it firm. Then he said something that I did not understand, my translator looked at me and said three words, "Leave him alone!"

Frustrated that he thought I was in the wrong, I said "What do you mean, leave *him* alone? I'm not doing anything to him! He is messing with me." The man let go of me. I lift my leg once again and that time it was the translator who pulled my leg down, "Don't show anyone the bottom of your foot. It's very disrespectful!"

He spoke to the man next to me. As they talked to one another, my head turned back and forth like I was watching a tennis match. Finally, my translator looked at me. He said, "He would like to apologize for touching you and hopes you can forgive him!"

"Please tell him it is I who would like to apologize. Just because I did not know did not make it right."

They spoke again for a few minutes. Then he turned to me and said, "He would like to invite you and your family to his house for dinner to show that there are no hard feelings. He has given me his number so that your uncle can call."

The train stopped and the man stood. My translator pulled me to my feet as well. The stranger turned to me and bowed. "Turn and bow to him!" my translator said.

As I bowed, he turned and stepped off the train. I sat back down as the train pulled off thinking quietly, how could this man whom I unknowingly disrespected forgive me and then invite me and my family to his house for dinner with his family? That was all I could think of for the last 20 minutes of the train ride.

As the translator and I made our way back to the base, I began to hope that my uncle and aunt would agree to go to his house for dinner. When we got back to my uncles, I started talking the minute I walked in the door. I told him everything that happened and asked if we could please go to his place. The moment I stopped talking, he picked up the phone and called the man. They spoke on the phone for some time about . . . who knows what? there was a little smiling and laughing.

Once he hung up, he informed me that we would be at his place for dinner that following Friday. For all the days leading up to that day, all I thought about is how this man, this stranger, had taught me a valuable lesson. Someone can be disrespected, but it does not have to be a big deal. When all is said and done, there is no need to have hard feelings. It's easy to forgive.

M I K E   S E V E R S O N

The Pebble

My son arrived into this world on his own schedule. He was born a week and a half after his mother's water broke. His pursuit of independence began before he came to be. He has always had a mind of his own.

About a year later, with my son still on teetering legs, I took him and his sister to the park. This playground was expansive. The jungle gym was every color of the rainbow, made of eco-friendly plastics and epoxy-covered steel beams and poles. Not a square corner in sight. The rack of chainy swings was enough to hold all the Rockettes and their leg-pumping splendor. Twisty and bumpy slides and crawling tubes to infinity, climbing walls and monkey bars endless enough to ensure premature greying to all the mothers whose children frequented this outdoor deathtrap. However, it was a paradise in the mind of a young child.

The playground was a part of the apartments that his mother managed. Her office overlooked the entire field of play and she had an unobstructed view down into it. Three feet of concrete surrounded the huge park. To soften any falls, trips, or follies in play . . . You guessed it, gravel. Guaranteed to get *everywhere* and stay stuck in your shoes until you grabbed a stick to dig it out. One would walk out of a play session sounding like Fred Astaire doing a tap dance routine.

Leading down to this Eden of play, six concrete stairs covered in, of course . . . gravel. My son, so independent and wanting to join his sister in play, just couldn't wait for help down the stairs. He started to fuss and tugged his hand from mine. Still being young myself and understanding

249

his need for freedom, I let go. Plus, there was the thought that flashed in my mind, "If you don't want my help, then just go you little shit." I soon regretted that sentiment.

With my son just a year old and the steps being as tall as they are, just didn't really match up. His legs were just about as long as the stairs were tall. So, when he took his first unassisted step, his foot never reached the next stair. His head was the next point of contact in his trip down. He ended up at the bottom of the stairs, eyes wide open and staring off into the sky looking every bit as dazed as I was scared. I rushed down and scooped him up before he could sound the alarm that every mother instinctually hears. I started to laugh, hoping that he'd realize that everything was ok, and it was still playtime. I looked down and gaped at the amount of gravel that was on his face. It was stuck to his snotty nose, his slobbering lips and even his fine, almost invisible hair. This was quite the trick, seeing as he didn't leave much there.

In cleaning off this magical gravel, I noticed that one pebble was stubbornly hanging onto my son's head. Thinking nothing of it, I plucked it off. You would've thought that I uncorked the hoover dam. His face was instantly covered in a brilliant red mask. Who knew someone who weighed less than 25 pounds could hold that much blood in him? The removal of the offending pebble and the alarm sounding were simultaneous, with super-human speed, his mother appeared by our side, freaking out sounding as if she was the one with tiny rocks embedded in her face. I could think of nothing else to do except plug the gushing hole with my thumb, tear him away from his mom's gripping hands and rush him into the bathroom to wash his face off. With his mother attached to my hip, it was next to impossible to get him to calm down.

After all the blood was washed off and circulating down the drain, all the worries about death went after it. We were all soon laughing about his new scar over ice cream and discussing our next trip to the park. Even though he survived, that one pebble taught me a very valuable dad lesson. No matter what kids think, they *do* need their parents' help. Even if they don't want it.

A N T H O N Y   S H A P I R O

Drumming with Dad

Ah! There it is again...The ceremonial intro on guitar reverberates—and yet soothes me. "Diary of a Madman" by Ozzy Osbourne must be one of my dad's favorite songs because he plays it quite often. I like it too. That reverberation shakes the flesh around me. Baby's First Rattle? The haunting feel of the song overall makes a great marriage to that intro. Not so sure if my mother likes it or not because sometimes she will complain that I'm kicking her too hard. But rock 'n' roll gets me a rocking and rollin'. The music is fluid to my soul, just as my soul is nourished by the fluid. What my mommy doesn't realize is those "kicks," as she puts it, are just me practicing for my career as a drummer.

I can't wait to get out of my mommy's tummy and delve deeper into the musical catalogs of bands like Led Zeppelin, Dio and Rush. Rush's drummer is the reason I want to play. He sounds so awesome! I think he came out of his mommy's tummy with four arms and four legs. If I am half the drummer he is, I will at least be the second best! I just want to make my dad proud because he is the driving force behind my choice of career. And what better way to make him proud than to make him an album buying, concert going, fan of my band! Wait, on second thought, I'll just give him a job as a roadie, so he can go to all of my concerts! His taste in music has really rubbed off on me this past eight months, and I want him to know how much that means to me.

I gotta go now. Dad has just put on Van Halen's "Eruption." Yet another guitar intro that shakes me to the core. Maybe I should play guitar?

S T E V E   S P I E S S

We Keep Walking

We move in a wedge formation through the frozen cedars. Breath rises in clouds in front of our silent, camo-painted faces. Permanent artillery pieces jut from the hills above to mirror their opposition north of the border. In the distance, two tall hills are topped by wooden observation towers that look for all the world like forest fire lookouts back home. Only these cast their shadows on unseen trenches and bunkers with 50 cal. placements behind sandbags and camo nets, connected to an underground barracks. A cruel, glistening coil of razor wire tops a ten-foot-tall fence, denying even a tattered plastic bag access to the other side; it forms the demarcation line.

PFC Kim is on point.

We keep walking.

On the other side is an entire fake town, "Propaganda Village." It's a collection of empty pink and turquoise and yellow buildings, like a Looney Toons movie set. It's there to show us how grand life could be if we crossed to the other side. So are the fluttering leaflets dropped from planes on south bound winds, showing cartoons of The Supreme Leader in bed with five women. So are the speakers, spaced along the fence and blasting current hits by Van Halen or Madonna or Bon Jovi to show us the bad guys like music, too. And so is the seventy-foot statue of the First Supreme Leader, Kim Il-Sung. Somehow, we manage to resist all of these charms and stay on our side.

A pheasant glides across an opening in the trees, and we keep walking.

My position as medic is with the RTO (radioman) and platoon leader at the center-rear of the wedge, so I hear the radio crackle to life. We halt as Wilson passes the handset to the L.T. who talks briefly with an intelligence officer in one of the towers. Most take the opportunity to remove gloves and blow life into our dying fists. When we move again, it's at an angle away from the fence, probably to avoid an enemy patrol on the other side. Kim takes us on a route that places a low berm between us and the fence. Michael Jackson can barely be heard singing behind us.

Then he's gone. We keep walking.

We move out of the trees onto a narrow road, and split into two single-file columns, one on either side of the road. A humming sound builds somewhere. The noise could be absolutely anything in the Alice-in-Wonderland twilight zone. Maybe a helicopter, Humvee, a swarm of giant purple mosquitos, or a lone killer clown on a moped. The reality is nothing so predictable. Past the checkpoints, the machine gun nests, the minefields, comes a convoy of black limousines. Sky-blue United Nations flags flutter from both sides as generals, ambassadors and politicians ride in heated, leather, window-tinted luxury past our muddy, frostbitten, bewildered faces. They disappear around a curve on their way to the conference building that straddles the line between yin and yang, where they'll argue the fate of this icy peninsula.

The hum fades into frigid silence, and we keep walking.

Phosphorus Flowers

"Are you sure this thing's safe?" I asked halfway up.

It was on a warm summer night that I reluctantly climbed this old wobbly ladder toward the stars.

"Oh, come on, it's fine." My dad replied dismissively from above.

He didn't say it in a rude way. He was always a really nice guy. He was just always kind of careless. Well, that's not true; maybe I was always just overly cautious. I got to the top and navigated the tricky transition from ladder to rooftop, worried about stepping in the gutter, or shifting my weight the wrong way and falling.

"Hurry up. They're going to start soon," he said. He was already laying comfortably on his back, hands behind his head, facing to the east where the fireworks would come from. Afraid to just stand up and walk, I crawled ever-so-carefully across the shingles. I thought that maybe if I crawled, I could disperse my weight better, and have less of a chance of falling through the roof. I sat right next to him and unloaded a small stash of Mountain Dew cans I had brought in my cargo pockets.

It was the 24th of July. If you're not from Utah, you probably won't know about Pioneer Day. Utah is so awesome; it has a second Fourth of July on the 24th. We call it Pioneer day, celebrating the pioneers that first settled in Utah.

We laid back on the roof, sippin' ice-cold sodas in anticipation, conjuring up old memories.

"Hey Dad, remember that time we took a family vacation to Las

Vegas when we were little? After we checked into the hotel you went down to the ATM and realized we had no money," I asked chuckling softly.

"Yeah," he answered with a grin. "Then I had to call Grandma to wire us some money, so we could at least have something to eat for the week."

"I remember eating peanut butter sandwiches in our hotel room. Best vacation ever!" I replied watching the memories of the Las Vegas Strip form in the night sky.

Somewhere in the memories the fireworks began. Boom, crackle, pop! I remember the little whizzing sound as a small spark shot into the sky. It faded in and out, and then there was a brief silence in the darkness. Only for a fraction of a second, the little ascending spark was lost in the stars, and then...boom! If you're close enough you can almost feel the loud ones, or a bright flash for the brilliant ones that showered light on the face of the person next to you, or the ones that popped and then popped again unexpectedly like a phosphorus flower growing new fluorescent pedals.

"Wow, did you see that one?" I asked. "Yeah, I like the ones that go up really high," he replied.

"Hey where's Janae?" I ask. Janae was his new girlfriend that had been hanging around a lot. She liked him but he didn't like to acknowledge it. I assumed he still felt it wasn't right to start dating again since mom passed away, but it had been seven years. At some point you have to cut yourself some slack.

"I need a break from her. I am pretty sure she's just using me," he replied.

I felt content in that moment, even though deep down I knew I would be going to prison soon. In my younger days, I would have done anything not to be stuck at home on a night like that. I would have been out partying with girls or smoking pot, but that night I was just happy sitting around spending time with my dad.

I thought to myself, isn't it funny: life's kind of like a firework. You go shooting up into the sky so fast, a little spark you can barely keep track of amongst the stars. We're so busy just trying to get here or there, or become someone, or rise up above everyone else that we lose focus. Then just for a moment, it burns out at the top, and we completely lose sight of it all. In the silence and darkness, you wonder, "Where am I? How did I get here? What was I thinking?" Then, boom! You feel it in your chest, it hits you like a ton of bricks: the beauty, the brilliance. The faces next to you become illuminated in the dark, and you realize who and what is actually important. It all suddenly becomes so obvious, but it's too short, too late. It all comes crashing down to the ground in a smoldering heap of ashes and sparks, and it all fades away. The memories, only fragments of light burned into the back of our eyelids fade with time. We lose track of people. They stop answering your calls. We forget. We move on. It's ok though, once again, we begin to rise up from the ashes, like the next firework.

"You have a prepaid call from an inmate at Sterling Correctional Facility if you—" Beep.

"Hey Dad. How's it going?" I say into the receiver.

"Good. What's up, son?"

"Not much. Hey, question for ya. Do you remember that night we laid out on the roof, drinking Mountain Dews and watching fireworks for the 24th?'

"Oh. No, I don't. Why?"

RICHARD VAN DER VOORT

Immolation

Uncontrollable, undeniable, unwavering reverence. Life consuming reverence. A reverence so strong that nothing else exists. There is only reverence—reverence for light. Reborn from the darkness into the darkness. Awakened with ravenous instinctual hunger. Not a hunger derived from the body—the body was meant for sacrifice. A hunger derived from the soul. A hunger for reverence, for the light.

Take to light, stirred by the myriad fluttering of Rorschach wings. A chrysalid hegira guide by some unseen force. Moved by the nocturnal hand of Dianna as she glows luminous and full, from the midnight heavens.

If only to touch her. The eternal reach in hopes of grasping even some facsimile to share in some verisimilitude of her true light.

And so, it is open flames that sings its siren song, the silk thread line separating salvation from perdition.

But reverence has no reservations, no questions, no hesitations. Bathe in the fire. Breath it in. Wear it as a cloak of angelic triumph as it consumes and destroys. Crashing like Icarus to the earth and entered into a yet new darkness.

Let a thousand darknesses descend! Stand me, impervious, through an eon of night. For through my reverence and grace, I have touched the light.

Black in a Golden Morning

Something or some things, were trying to destroy me in a way nothing else in the world could have, on this deeply-inspirational, golden-lit summer morning in Denver. These mornings are a must-see even for night owls. I woke physically limber, but so mentally distraught it took every fiber of my being to not break down right here on the gum-infested sidewalk as I waited for the light rail at Auraria Campus, six car lanes and a median away from a mini strip mall. The Burger King, Starbucks, Subway, Cricket phone store and everything else was showered in a soft golden filter. I've always battled my goliath moments of depression as David and won by the skin of my teeth, only because my depression is based on circumstances and not chemical imbalances.

The moments I'm most depressed—like this 100-karat-gold morning with a hotdog vendor, graffiti-laden bus stop, blue skies and no wind—every guy is a friendly motor mouth, every woman that normally isn't, is audacious enough to conversationally weave between my legs like a flirtatious car and every wild animal is domesticated enough to invade my personal space. If I could, I'd pay a million dollars to go to a private soundproof room and cry all the fluids and bad blood out of me leaving a puddle of pain, misery and anxiety. The traffic on Colfax is loud, irritating and full of pollution (people's cigs don't help) and it shatters the golden ambiance of tranquility. So I put in my headphones, and these rappers amplify my depression. I knew I should have got more instrumentals, because they're rapping about everything anyone wants, but I can't stand listening to the obnoxious dodo bird walk signal for pedestrians, the roaring engines of busses with stupid food ads on the side, car horns, screeching tires, Spanish, arguments, pigeon coos, sparrow twitters, or the light rails with their loud doors, A/C, bells and whistles and repetitive annoying female voice recordings. So I let Tech N9ne and Lil Wayne tell me what I'll never have or do.

Step by step, the dark tomb of my psyche and spirit engulfs me, as I find a soft-colored striped seat on the light rail. The world is halfway distorted and golden through piles of tears on my bottom eyelids. My jaw is clenched and I'm debating on letting out the floor in front of this beautiful twenty-something-year-old woman in pink with blue eyes and blonde hair who tried to converse with me in cat-like fashion on the gum-infested sidewalk, but I ignored because I had to focus on hiding tears back, she won't stop smiling and staring at me and avoiding eye contact is overwhelming and now I remember when someone I loved stared at me like that. I remember a massive junkyard of bittersweet memories all at one and I'm nanoseconds away from unleashing the tsunami as my tears and throat and neck build with sorrowful pressure, the kind of pressure only crying releases. To distract myself from melancholy, I make eye contact with her and briefly wonder if she's the type to like my tears like a demon, kiss them away like an angel. Then I wonder what the hell is the expression on my face leading her to not understand I'm in a state of anguish. Am I masking it well? In my head I feel like I'm being ripped apart and discarded. Sparrows are having a picnic as the light rail pulls away. Distorted green leafy trees on my right, Auraria's brick and mortar on my left. Everything still veiled in soft bright gold.

Then, finally, Pearl Jam's "Black" comes on. I'm looking out the light rail window watching a blurry gold world go by when I hear "WOOOAAAOOHHH." My watery eyes hold back the tsunami and I take in the deeply poetic verses as the guitar strums mend my ripped apart soul and release the built-up pressure. I can relate as it's about love, loss, redemption and how it's okay to have problems and not feel okay. This song has so much pain it pulls mine from my eyes, heart, and stomach, through my eardrums, to my headphones and into my iPhone. I let out deep breaths of relief and my stomach feels lighter. Closing the light, chasing my dreams. Capturing the sense of healing the song brings. Without this song, I don't know what I would have done on this deeply-inspirational, golden-lit summer morning. It held and fixed me in a way nothing else in the world could have.

Acknowledgments

A big thank you to the Colorado Department of Corrections' Programs and Education staff who went above and beyond to make the *Tell It Slant* course and anthology possible.

A special thanks to the following people without whose generous support DU PAI programming would not be possible:
    CDOC Executive Director, Dean Williams
    CDOC Public Information Officer, Annie Skinner
    CDOC Director of Prisons, Matt Hansen
    CDOC Education Team, Melissa Smith and Joan Carson

To these DU PAI *Tell It Slant* affiliate faculty, whose talent and heart as the course's instructors, helped inspire the skill and creativity exhibited in this book and beyond it: Libby Catchings, Diana Dresser, Tara Falk, Nicholle Harris, Reanna Magruder, Joan Dieter Mazza, Lars Reid, and Joanna Rotkin.

We're proud to acknowledge these DU PAI staff members dedicating countless hours to the Imagining Worlds course and anthology:
    Co-Facilitator of Course: Elijah N.
    Co-Facilitator of Course: Suzi Q. Smith
    Anthology Facilitation & Copyediting: Julie Rada
    Proofreading Support: Dan Manzanares
    Anthology Support: Tess Neel
    Book Design: Sonya Unrein

All proceeds of the *Tell It Slant* anthology will help to further support DU Prison Arts Initiative's arts-based workshops.

Tell It Slant: An Anthology of Creative Nonfiction by Writers from Colorado's Prisons is supported by Colorado Department of Corrections and is a publication of LuxLit Press.

Carve Magazine
Carve Magazine Submissions
PO Box 701510
Dallas, TX 75370

Cimarron Review
Cimarron Review
PO Box 210069
Cincinnati, OH 45221-0069

Clackamas Literary Review
Clackamas Literary Review
Clackamas Community College
19600 Molalla Ave.
Oregon City, OR 97045

Columbia Poetry Review
Columbia Poetry Review
Dept of Creative Writing
Columbia College Chicago
600 South Michigan
Ave Chicago, IL 60605

Conduit
CONDUIT.ORG

Confrontation
Confrontation Magazine, English Dept
LIU Post 720 Northern Blvd.
Brookville, NY 11548

Conjunctions
Bradford Morrow, Editor
Conjunctions 21 E 10th St. # 3E
New York, NY 10003

Crab Orchard Review
Southern Illinois University
Carbondale Department of English
1000 Fanner Dr Mail Code 4503
Carbondale, IL 62901

Cream City Review
Poetry/Fiction Contest Editor
Cream City Review
University of Wisconsin
Milwaukee Dept. of English
PO Box 413
Milwaukee, WI 53201

Creative Nonfiction
Creative Nonfiction Magazine
5119 Coral St.
Pittsburgh, PA 15224

Cutthroat, A Journal of the Arts
Cutthroat Journal Submissions
Cutthroat Literary Award
PO Box 2414
Durango, CO 81302

December Magazine
December Magazine
PO Box 16130
St. Louis, MO 63105

Denver Quarterly
Denver Quarterly
University of Denver
Dept. of English
2000 E. Asbury
Denver, CO 80208

Fantasy and Science Fiction Magazine
C.C. Finlay - Editor
The Magazine of Fantasy and Science Fiction
PO Box 8420
Surprise, AZ 85374

Florida Review
FLORIDAREVIEW.CAH.UCF.EDU
Online only

Fourth Genre
Fourth Genre-SUBMISSION Room 235
Bessey Hall Michigan State University 434
Farm Lane East Lansing, MI 48824

Gallery Press Ireland
GALLERYPRESS.COM
The Gallery Press
Loughcrew
Oldcastle
County Meath
Ireland

Gemini Magazine
Gemini Magazine
PO Box 1485
Onset, MN 02558

Georgia Review
UGA.EDU/GAREV
Editor, The Georgia Review
706A Main Library
320 S Jackson St
University of Georgia
Athens, GA 30602-9009

Gettysburg Review
GETTYSBURGREVIEW.COM
Mark Drew, Editor
The Gettysburg Review
Gettysburg College
300 N Washington St
Gettysburg, PA 17325-1491

Glimmer Train
Glimmer Train Press, Inc.
PO Box 80430
Portland, OR 97280-1430

Gulf Coast
Gulf Coast Literary Journal
4800 Calhoun Rd
Houston, TX 77204-3013

Hanging Loose Magazine
Hanging Loose Magazine
231 Wyckoff St.
Brooklyn, NY 11217

Harvard Review
Editors, Harvard Review
Lamont Library Harvard University
Cambridge, MA 02138

Hawai'I Review
Hawai'i Review
Hemenway Hall 107 2445 Campus Rd
Honolulu, HI 96822

Hudson Review
Editors, Hudson Review
33 W 67th St.
New York, NY 10023

I-70 Review
I-70 Review
913 Joseph Dr.
Lawrence, KS 66049

Indiana Review
Indiana Review
Indiana University
Ballantine Hall 529
1020 E Kirkwood Ave.
Bloomington, IN 47405-7103

Intergalactic Medicine Show
INTERGALACTICMEDICINESHOW.COM
Online only

Iowa Review
[Fiction, CNF, Poetry] Editor
The Iowa Review
308 EPB University of Iowa
Iowa City, IA 52242

Lake Effect Journal
Lake Effect
School of Humanities and Social Sciences
Penn State, Erie
The Behrend College
4951 College Dr
Erie, PA 16563-1501

Laurel Review
LAURELREVIEW.ORG
The Laurel Review
Greentower Press
Dept of Language, Literature and Writing
Northwest Missouri State University
800 University Dr
Maryville, MO 64468

Mid American Review
Mid-American Review
Dept of English
Bowling Green State University
Bowling Green, OH 43403

Midwest Quarterly
Casie Hermansson, Editor-in-Chief or
Lori Martin, Poetry Editor
Midwest Quarterly
Pittsburg State University
1701 S. Broadway
Pittsburg, KS 66762

Mississippi Review
Mississippi Review Contest – YEAR
118 College Dr #5144
Hattiesburg, MS 39406-0001

Missouri Review
[Genre] Editor: The Missouri Review
357 McReynolds Hall
University of Missouri
Columbia, MO 65211

The Nation
POEMNATIONSUBMIT@GMAIL.COM

Natural Bridge
Natural Bridge
Dept of English University of Missouri
St Louis One University Blvd
St. Louis, MO 63121

New England Review
(Give reason for mailed submission in cover
letter, i.e., no internet access)
New England Review Middlebury College
Middlebury, VT 05753

New Issues Poetry & Prose
New Issues Poetry and Prose
Western Michigan University
1903 West Michigan Ave
Kalamazoo, MI 49008-5463

Nimrod International Journal
Nimrod International Journal
University of Tulsa
800 S Tucker Dr
Tulsa, OK 74104

Normal School
THENORMALSCHOOL.COM
Online only

Paris Review
[Genre] Editor Paris Review
544 W 27th St.
New York , NY 10001

Phoebe
Attn: John Guthrie, Phoebe Journal
MSN 2C5 George Mason University
4400 University Dr.
Fairfax, VA 22030

Pinyon
Pinyon Review Submissions
23847 V66 Trail
Montrose, CO 81403

Pleiades
Pleiades Dept of English Martin 336
University of Central Missouri
415 E Clark St.
Warrensburg, MO 64093

Ploughshares
Ploughshares Emerson College
120 Boylston St.
Boston, MA 02116-4624

Poet Lore
Poet Lore c/o The Writer's Center
4508 Walsh St.
Bethesda, MD 20815

Poetry
POETRYFOUNDATION.ORG
online only

Prairie Schooner
Prairie Schooner
110 Andrews Hall
Lincoln, NE68588-0334

Prism International
Kyla Jamieson, Prose Editor OR
Shazia Hafiz Ramji, Poetry Editor
Prism International Journal
Creative Writing Program
UBC Buch E462-1866 Main Mall
Vancouver , BC V6T 1Z1 Canada

Puerto Del Sol
PUERTODELSOL.ORG
Online only

Rattle
Rattle
12411 Ventura Blvd
Studio City, CA 91604

River Styx
River Styx Magazine
3139A South Grand Blvd suite 203
St Louis, MO 63118

River Teeth
River Teeth Beautiful Things
Attn: Cassandra Brown
401 College Ave
Bixler Hall, room 105
Ahland, OH 44805

Salamander
Salamander Suffolk University
English Department 8 Ashburton Place
Boston, MA 02108

Santa Monica Review
Santa Monica Review
Santa Monica College
1900 Pico Blvd
Santa Monica, CA 90405

Saranac Review
Saranac Review
Dept of English
101 Broad St.
Plattsburgh, NY 12901

Seattle Review
SEATTLEREVIEW.ORG
Online Only

Seneca Review
Seneca Review
Hobart and William Smith Colleges
300 Pulteney St
Geneva , NY 14456

Sewanee Review
Sewanee Review
735 University Ave
Sewanee, TN

Shenandoah
Shenandoah Washington and Lee University
Lexington, VA 24450

Slant
Slant - A Journal of Poetry
University of Central Arkansas
PO Box 5063
201 Donaghey Ave,
Conway, AR 72035-5000

Slipstream Magazine
Slipstream Poetry [Contest]
PO Box 2071
Niagara Falls, NY 14301

SQ Magazine
SQMAG.COM
Online submissions only

Southern Humanities Review
CLA.AUBURN.EDU
Online only

Southern Review
The Southern Review
338 Johnston Hall
Baton Rouge, LA 70803

South West Review
Southwest Review
PO Box 750374
Dallas, TX 75275-0374

Sow's Ear Poetry
Krista Camitta Zimet, Editor
Sow's Ear Poetry Review
308 Greenfield Ave.
Winchester, VA 22602
Additional Address for Contests
Sara Kohrs, Managing Editor
Sow's Ear Poetry Review
1748 Cave Ridge Rd.
Mount Jackson, VA 22842

Space and Time Magazine
SPACEANDTIMEMAGAZINE.COM
Online only

Spoon River Poetry Review
Spoon River Poetry Review
Illinois State University
4241 English Dept.
Normal, IL61790-4241

Strange Horizons
STRANGEHORIZONS.COM
Online submissions system

Sugar House Review
SUGARHOUSEREVIEW.COM
Sugar House Review
PO Box 13
Cedar City, UT 84721

Tallgrass Literary Review
TALLGRASSREVIEW.COM
Tallgrass Publishing
PO Box 1866
Owasso, OK 74055

The Sun
THESUNMAGAZINE.ORG/ABOUT
SUBMISSION_GUIDELINES/WRITING
Editorial Dept
The Sun
107 N Roberson St
Chapel Hill, NC 27516

Threepenny Review
THREEPENNYREVIEW.COM
Editors, Threepenny Review
PO Box 9131
Berkeley, CA 94709

Tin House
tinhouse.com
Online only

Tiny Lights
TINY-LIGHTS.COM
Tiny Lights Publications
PO Box 928
Petaluma, CA 94953

Water~Stone Review
WATERSTONEREVIEW.COM
Water-Stone Review Submissions
MS-A1730
1536 Hewitt Ave
St Paul, MN 55104

Wisconsin Review
UWOSH.EDU/WISCONSINREVIEW
Wisconsin Review
Submissions
University of Wisconsin Oshkosh
800 Algoma Blvd
Oshkosh, WI 54901

Xavier Review
xula.edu/review
Ralph Adamo, radamo@xula.edu

Yale Review
YALE.EDU/YALEREVIEW
Yale Review
Yale University
PO Box 208243
New Haven, CT 06520-8243

Zoetrope: All-Story
ALL-STORY.COM
Zoetrope: All-Story
Attn: Fiction Editor
916 Kearny St
San Francisco, CA 94133

LUXLIT PRESS.

LuxLit Press is the publishing venture of the Denver University Prison Arts Initiative (DU PAI). We are an intentional collaboration inside and out of prisons in the state of Colorado. *LuxLit* is designed to spark new understandings for people anywhere, through the publication of original materials created by people who are incarcerated. It is our mission to cultivate relationships with authors and artists (creators) by generating spaces for education and dialogue thereby doing more than just crafting outstanding art, but seeing, supporting and strengthening every creator we come into contact with. *LuxLit* is publishing a wide variety of genres and platforms including *The Inside Report* and *Reverberations The Magazine*. This provides opportunities to produce strong literary and visual art, as well as to discover previously untapped resources within the incarcerated community.

Made in the USA
Monee, IL
03 December 2023

48045701R00166